The Role of Knowledge in Western Religion

John Herman Randall, Jr. is Woodbridge Professor of Philosophy in Columbia University, where he has been teaching since 1918. He is author of *The Making of the Modern Mind, Our Changing Civilization,* and *Nature and Historical Experience.* With his father he wrote *Religion and the Modern World.* He is the coauthor of many works, including *The Theology of Paul Tillich,* and has written extensively about philosophy, intellectual history, and religion. Mr. Randall has served as president of the Eastern Division of the American Philosophical Association and of the Renaissance Society of America, and as chairman of the editorial committee of *The Journal of the History of Ideas.* He is a joint editor of *The Journal of Philosophy,* and a fellow of the American Academy of Arts and Sciences.

The Role of Knowledge

in Western Religion

John Herman Randall, Jr.

Starr King Press   Beacon Hill   Boston

Horatio Leland Friess

Magistro Dilectissimo et Amico

Qui Semper Quid Faciendum Scit

Contents

Foreword

This volume owes its preparation to the Mead-Swing Lecture Foundation of Oberlin College, founded "to keep Oberlin students informed of significant developments in science, in religion, and in the relations between the two fields." The invitation to speak at Oberlin came in the most persuasive way possible. It was extended on behalf of the Mead-Swing Lecture Committee in a letter from my old friend Walter M. Horton, whose office I shared during my first year of college teaching at Columbia. It was one of the many gratifications of my stay at Oberlin in October, 1955, to have had the chance to observe at first hand that Professor Horton enjoys the same intellectual distinction and leadership on his own illustrious campus that I had long known he had won throughout the Church, and the universal affection of colleagues and students alike. He spared no effort to make my visit both comfortable and stimulating, and I remain deeply indebted to the hospitality of the adventurous comrade of my youth.

For their unremitting kindness and their penetrating philosophical discussion I must also thank the members of the Oberlin Department of Philosophy, William E. Kennick (now of Amherst), Paul F. Schmidt, and Frances W. Herring, whose friendship I have cherished since a winter spent in Seattle. And to Frederick B. Artz I owe unforgettable memories of several illuminating conversations I was privileged to hold with him in his home, a treasure house of medieval art.

This volume would have been quite impossible without the stimulus, the incentive, and the wise interpretations of Arthur Cushman McGiffert, the best lecturer on the Columbia campus during my student days, who inspired me with a lasting interest in the history of Christian thought, and taught me most of what I have ever learned and little I have ever had to unlearn about that fascinating subject.

John Herman Randall, Jr.

Peacham, Vermont
July, 1958

The Role of Knowledge in Western Religion

Introduction. *From Conflict to Problem*

When I was originally asked to speak under the pleasant aus-
pices of the Mead-Swing Lecture Foundation at Oberlin College,
the theme proposed was, "Religion and Science in their Historical
Relations." What such a title would have suggested a generation
or two ago we all know. It would have pointed to an historical
treatment of the burning intellectual issue in religion in those days,
the problem of "the conflict between science and theology." The
vital question then was, "Has 'science' disproved this or that
religious belief?"

An historical treatment would have taken one of two forms.
On the one hand, it might have concentrated on the familiar tradi-
tional episodes, in which the ecclesiastical authorities, relying on
the civil power, made immortal martyrs out of men who stood for
new scientific ideas—among other things. It would have dwelt on
Bruno, the infinite worlds, and the stake in the Campo dei Fiori.
It would have driven home Galileo, his bitter recantation, and his
apocryphal "E pur si muove." It would then have moved down to
Darwin, Bishop Wilberforce, and the monkey grandmother of
Thomas Huxley. The classic expression of such a one-sided
chronicle is *The History of the Warfare of Science with Theology*
(1896) of that doughty apostle of scientific education, Andrew
D. White.

On the other hand, the treatment might have labored to show
that there is not and never has been any conflict between science
and religion, "rightly understood." The late nineteenth-century
impression that there had been and still was one, was all a mistake.
The historical demonstration would have taken as its text John
Fiske's "Evolution is God's way of doing things." It would have
shown how in the West Christian doctrine has been repeatedly
formulated in terms of the best science of the day. It would have

1

appealed to the intellectual Doctors of the ancient Greek Church, rather than to the unscientific Latin Fathers; and to the great medieval Aristotelians. It would have quoted Thomas Aquinas: "Between true faith and true science there can be no conflict, for both come from God." It would have ended with a plea for translating into the Christian language the best evolutionary philosophy and ethics of the times. Of such a policy of appeasing science, classic American expressions are not only John Fiske's evolutionary theism, but also Lyman Abbott's *The Theology of an Evolutionist* (1897), and the *Reconstruction in Theology* (1900) of that honest and influential apostle of liberal religion at Oberlin, Henry Churchill King.

Neither of these two treatments, so popular half a century ago, would be intellectually or religiously possible today. Both attitudes, in fact, seem to us curiously remote. For nothing is more alien to our own experience than the problems which exercised our fathers' generation. The issues themselves do indeed have a way of persisting: the relations between science and religion certainly form a major question for us today, at least for those of us who have a vital concern with both these great human enterprises. But though that be true, at least the way our immediate predecessors formulated those problems strikes us today as utterly perverse.

Few today, outside the definitely old-fashioned, any longer believe there is an essential "conflict between science and religion," or even between "science and theology"—though most of us would be hard put to it to offer any reasoned explanation of just why. We recognize there have been and are plenty of specific conflicts between new scientific ideas, like the evolutionary concepts that so upset our fathers, and older religious beliefs. Or rather, we have come to suspect, they have usually been between new and better scientific ideas and older scientific ideas that happened to become enshrined as religious beliefs. Since the very function of science is to change men's beliefs, there will always be such conflicts. But we have learned they are quite incidental to the essential functioning of religion.

We have also come to recognize that psychological incompatibilities between scientific and religious attitudes are probably far more important than logical conflicts. For, we have learned, there are no two ideas, no matter how contradictory they may appear on the surface, which, if there be strong motives for maintaining both, the wit of man cannot "reconcile" intellectually. The trick has been turned again and again, by modernist theologians and philosophers of religion. But psychological incompatibilities can strike at and weaken our very motives for wanting to believe. In this "scientific" and technological age of ours, curious things have been happening to the status and appeal of religion, as to those of other nonscientific enterprises like art and poetry.

On the other hand, there are few today who would hold that religious beliefs can be simply identified with scientific ideas and that we can find a satisfactory theology, or an adequate notion of God, in any of the concepts of any of our sciences. And there are not even many who would and can make a living religious faith out of a scientific philosophy, that is, a philosophy that generalizes fundamental scientific concepts, or, as is more common today, gives philosophic expression to the scientific attitude and method. If there be no longer any basic "conflict" between science and religion, still less is there the temptation to assume an identity of content or function.

What is the source of this changed attitude of ours, which makes both the issue of "the conflict between science and religion" and that of their "reconciliation" seem such unreal problems for us, and to strike us as so obviously missing the point? The answer is clear: in our deepened understanding, we have come to have a very different conception of the role of knowledge and truth in religion. The place we now assign to all intellectual factors in the functioning of the religious life—to doctrine, belief, truth, intelligence itself—has since the end of the nineteenth century been profoundly modified. In that age the great problem was to assimilate a revolutionary science and effect an adjustment between it and the other institutions of culture, including religion. Since it was the beliefs that had come down in the religious tradition that furnished the chief obstacle to this intellectual assimilation of the new science, the element of belief and the claim to possess religious knowledge were naturally forced into a central prominence in religion itself. That prominence of belief we now realize was the product of a transitory cultural adjustment, and was in fact a great distortion of the essential nature and function of religious experience.

What are the causes of this revolutionary change in our conception of the role of knowledge and truth in religion? At bottom of course, the shift is a tribute to the success of the adjustment our fathers' generation effected. With religious "truth" no longer competing with scientific "knowledge," other problems, emphasizing quite different factors in religion than beliefs, have come to arrest the attention of thoughtful religious men. But very important also is all that we have learned about the nature and function of religion itself, from the philosophic and scientific study and analysis of human experience and its great cultural enterprises. That complex story we must reserve for our third chapter. But here we must recognize that the most significant effect of science upon religion has come from the scientific study of religion itself. And whatever is left of major conflict between the two today is no longer between a scientific and a religious treatment of the universe or even of human life, but between a scientific and a religious treatment of religion. The issue today lies between the scientific understanding of religion, elaborated in various philosophical interpretations, and the conception of religion shared in common in the divergent interpretations offered by traditional, liberal, and radical and anticlerical religious thought. The really revolutionary effect of science upon religion has in the long run turned out to be not its newer views of the world, or even of man, but its new views of religion: of what religion is and does in human life.

Both religion and science, we have come to recognize, are

things men do: they are human activities. And men do them together with their fellows: they are social activities, organized and
institutionalized ways of acting, aspects of group behavior, traits of
the culture of that group. Like all the institutions of a society, these
religious and scientific ways of acting themselves do something; they
perform certain functions. And they incidentally do something to
each other, as well as to all the other institutions, especially when
they are changing. But the cultural functions of religion and of
science are so different that it is difficult to see how, despite their
incidental reactions on each other, they can seriously compete.
Both functions are clearly indispensable. For the individual, of
course, this is not true. This or that man can get along without religion, or without science, or without both—multitudes have always
managed to, and do today. But no society can dispense with
either. Religion is doubtless culturally more necessary than
science, for few cultures, until very recently, have ever developed
any science, while none has been without religion. Recent experience makes clear that, if a traditional religion disintegrates, a
new one will spring up to fill the vacuum, and to perform the essential traditional functions. And it will be much worse than the
old, for it will express a need of the moment, it will be one sided
and fanatical. It will have forgotten so much, because it lacks the
clarification and criticism of centuries of experience.

Religion is indispensable for any society. But science is also
indispensable for any modern society. Now it would be strange
were there a basic conflict in general between two socially necessary
and essential functions. There can of course be plenty of conflict
between particular ways of behaving religiously and particular ways
of behaving scientifically at any one time. There can be specific
intellectual conflicts. What men believe when they are acting
religiously may be wholly at variance with what they believe
when they are acting scientifically. The former beliefs may be
judged by the standards of the latter enterprise to be mythology
or susperstition. But mythology is only superstition if it has
ceased to perform a religious function and is trying to serve as

pseudo science. "Myths" and "symbols," we have learned, have an essential and indispensable function of their own to perform in the enterprise of religion. There can also be specific psychological incompatibilities. The same man, and the same group, can have characteristic ways of acting scientifically, religiously, politically, and in many other fashions. To act in one way is not the same as to act in another. To pray to the Virgin or to light Friday candles is not to act scientifically. But neither is to listen to a symphony or to enjoy a painting or to cast a ballot or to go out on strike. For some men, one of these ways of acting may well crowd out others. They have no time and no appreciation for music, or they cannot get interested in the enjoyment of religion. For the individual, such competition doubtless exists. But rounded societies have provided for all these very human activities, and the great religions have consecrated all these persisting enterprises of man.

Religion, we now see, is a distinctive human enterprise with a socially indispensable function of its own to perform. It is not primarily a set of beliefs offering knowledge to men. It is not a kind of bastard science, whose superstitions are at war with scientific truths. Nor is it a kind of super-science proclaiming a "higher" form of knowledge forever beyond the reach of "mere science" and its crude laboratory methods. Religion is not essentially knowledge at all. Yet it clearly involves knowledge, many different kinds of knowledge. Christianity in particular was endowed by Greek thinkers with a complex philosophical theology, a set of propositions about God and his relation to man and to the world, which expressed their own faith in reason and knowing. This theology, though rarely understood and often taken in the West as a "mystery" to be accepted on faith, has enabled the Christian beliefs to serve as symbols for intellectual as well as moral values. In the Christian tradition, scientists and philosophers have again and again been able to express their devotion to intelligibility and knowledge and truth in Christian terms. And great Christian thinkers like Augustine and Thomas Aquinas have interpreted

"God" philosophically to mean "Truth"—that Truth which is the source of all other truths.

Here is a genuine intellectual problem. Just what is the role of knowledge and of truth in the enterprise of religion? What is their role in a living religious faith? We are agreed today that it cannot be what the nineteenth century, misled by its alarms and excursions over the irruption of a revolutionary science, mistakenly imagined it to be. But we are scarcely agreed on the answer we should ourselves now give. Fortunately, this seems to be a problem with which analysis and investigation can hope to make some headway. For the biggest change that has come over our continuing concern with the relations between science and religion has been the transformation of an issue to be endlessly debated into a problem that can be inquired into. It is in this spirit of inquiry that we shall examine the record of the Western religious tradition, in the hope that the experience of history will throw some light on our central problem.

The problem is complex enough, and in no religious tradition so intricate as in that of the Christian West. The intellectual elaborations it has there received indeed suggest that every possibility has been explored, that every conceivable position has at some time been tried out. Christianity, having acquired a subtle and philosophically profound theology, adopted elaborate creeds that claimed to set forth knowledge and to contain in fact the only saving "Truth." It also took form in the very home of ancient science and philosophy. It then came to be embraced by the one culture that first adopted Greek science, and then devised, in snowballing fashion, successive further forms of "science." This unique combination has made intellectual curiosity central in the Western tradition, and has provoked thoughtful Christians and Jews within it to a never-ending process of philosophical interpretation and reinterpretation, adjustment and reconciliation.

The greatest prophets tell us that religion is simple; and in the truest religious geniuses, in Jesus or Saint Francis or Buddha, it is profoundly simple indeed. But the religion of complex and subtle

men is inevitably subtle and complex, while the religion of elaborate and complicated cultures must develop complicated and elaborate forms. The Christianity that has come down to us has been
the product of generation after generation of men who, if not always intelligent, have at least in their interests been intellectual.
Truth and knowledge have been woven inextricably into its fine-
spun fabric.

Three main positions have been held in the West on the place
of knowledge and truth in the religious life. First, it has been maintained that Christianity proclaims as an essential part of its faith
a revelation of "truth," a set of beliefs enshrined in the Bible and
authoritatively interpreted in the historic creeds of the Church.
This religious knowledge is like all other knowledge: it is about the
world and man, and is to be judged by the rational standards that
are the test of any knowledge. Originally, the specific evidence for
its validity was "revelation," and no other and secular evidence to
the contrary could stand against it. But very soon the meaning of
"revealed" truth was in the West identified with an acceptable
philosophic scheme of understanding: religious "truth" must agree
with men's best knowledge of the world.

Secondly, it has been held that Christianity is indeed a revelation of truth, but this special "religious" knowledge is unlike all
other knowledge in that it deals with a "higher realm," a realm
inaccessible to rational inquiry and its methods; or with a quite different aspect of experience from other knowledge. Historically
this religious knowledge has been taken as "the truths propounded
by faith" in contrast to the truths accessible to man's "natural
reason," or as the truths belonging to the "realm of grace" rather
than to the "realm of nature." Since the time of Kant, its proper
object has often been held to be the "realm of values" with which
scientific methods cannot deal, as over against the "realm of fact"
which science has appropriate techniques for treating. Since the
rise of concern with a "religious experience" conceived as something quite unique with a distinctive object of its own, "religious"
knowledge has been held to be knowledge of the special and pecul-

iar object of this experience—that which the mystic's vision beholds, the "Holy" or the "Numinous," "Existential Truth."

Thirdly, and normally in reaction against the difficulties of these two positions, it has been held that religion in general, like Christianity in particular, offers men no independent "knowledge" at all, though it can give religious expression and consecration to the many kinds of knowledge and the many truths men can find in their experience of the world. Religion is a way of acting and feeling, not a way of knowing: it is practical and aesthetic rather than cognitive. Theology is not a theoretical but a "practical science," as Duns Scotus and William of Ockham put it. It is a description of "the religious consciousness," not of the nature of the world, as Schleiermacher expressed it. It is an imaginative and symbolic rendering of men's moral experience and ideals: all religious beliefs are symbolic, in Santayana's modern interpretation. Religious beliefs are not literal knowledge, but "symbols." And religious symbols are not cognitive; their function in the religious life is not to mediate truth, but to serve quite different ends. It is to clarify and strengthen a commitment, to stimulate religious vision, rather than to furnish knowledge and truth.

Of these three positions, it is the first which, by placing religious beliefs and knowledge on the same level as other knowledge, inevitably leads to conflicts with every new scheme of science. If to furnish an intellectual explanation of the world and of human life be taken as a major function of religion, and if Christianity maintain that man is saved only by holding the correct beliefs about God and man and human destiny, as orthodox Protestantism early came to hold, then the outcome is either an irrepressible conflict, or, in the longer run, the successive modification of those beliefs in the light of a changing and growing understanding of the world and of life. If true beliefs be essential to religion, any new knowledge or experience, just as for Protestants any new interpretation of the Scriptures, must be incorporated into religious faith.

Thus the end product of this first position, once the belief in the letter of revelation has been modified, is to identify religious faith completely with a set of "scientific" or philosophic propositions about the world as the scene of the moral life. In the eighteenth century this process succeeded in reducing religion to the three ideas of "rational theology": God, freedom, and immortality. In the nineteenth, it associated religion with the elaborate systems of philosophical idealism stemming from Hegel, who held that Christianity is really the expression in symbolic form of the truths he had succeeded in stating in exact and philosophic fashion. Still later it led to the identification of a humanistic "liberal religion" with the popular evolutionary philosophies. Since World War II, the main issue in Protestant theology in Germany has been presented by Rudolf Bultmann's program of *Entmythologisierung*— "getting rid of mythology"—which makes religious faith equivalent to acceptance of Heidegger's ontology. Many would hold that a like position is approached in this country by Paul Tillich.[1] Such has been the outcome of taking religion as a set of propositions to be believed, as essentially a body of true knowledge.

Since this is the consequence of placing religious knowledge on the same level as all other knowledge, subtle and reflective men have profited by this experience to adopt the second position. There is no "rational theology" drawing upon secular knowledge and scientific principles. Religious knowledge is unique and distinctive, with a proper object of its own. By carefully setting boundaries to the "realm" and to the competence of "reason" or science, an impregnable stronghold will still be left for religious truth. Science will then be wholly autonomous within its own field, and free from religious interference. This has made the second position very popular with scientists. But it will not be omnicompetent, and it will of necessity abandon all jurisdiction over reli-

---

[1] Actually, Mr. Tillich does not, like Bultmann, want to replace a mythological language with a moralistic one, but only to recognize the symbolic character of mythology. And his own existential philosophy is more dependent on Schelling, Nietzsche, and Kafka, while Bultmann's rests primarily on Kierkegaard and Heidegger. Above all, Mr. Tillich holds that while existentialism can raise the fundamental questions, it cannot of itself provide the answers.

gious beliefs. The first great Christian thinker who thus adjusted science and religion by assigning different fields to their respective forms of knowledge was Thomas Aquinas. The most influential modern philosopher to take this same way out was Immanuel Kant. This is probably the most widely accepted of the three positions held by thoughtful Christians today. It is expressed in countless forms, and in a multitude of theories of just what is the distinctive field of religious knowledge.

Unfortunately, this solution has never been able to maintain itself. Science and scientific methods have always refused to admit their limitations and to stay within their assigned boundaries. They have always pushed on into the forbidden fields reserved for religious knowledge. Each new attempt to set up an unassailable preserve for religious truth has had to surrender more territory than its predecessor. The efforts of theological Canutes have always failed. Moreover, such a position has always been felt to be profoundly unsatisfactory philosophically. The mind of man refuses to rest content with such a division between two different kinds of knowledge, and forever seeks to break down its watertight compartments. With regard to new scientific and religious truth, Christianity at least has never been able in the long run to practice closed communion: in the end the new knowledge has always been admitted to the table of the Lord.

The outcome of such intellectual experience has repeatedly driven candid and honest minds in the Western tradition to the third position: the enterprise of religion is not a form of knowledge at all; its aims and functions are not to furnish men truth. There can thus be no conflict in general between religion and science as explanations of anything, as truth. For whenever men are concerned with explanation and truth, they are acting theoretically or scientifically. To furnish such explanation is one of the distinctive functions of science, broadly conceived. Religion is no more a way of explaining anything than is artistic or political activity. That is not what they do; it is not their proper function. Even when men are explaining something in religion, or in art, they are engaged in what is essentially a scientific activity. Theology, conceived as an explanation of something—what has traditionally been called "rational theology"—is actually a scientific and philosophical, not a religious enterprise. And it is bound by the standards of scientific intelligibility and verification, carefully built up in the institutionalized science of our culture, and often condemned by them. Fortunately for theology, it has other and more important functions than explanation, genuinely religious functions.

The religion of a complex society, especially the religion of the subtle, the reflective and the learned, will normally express and consecrate intellectual and scientific values. It will naturally draw on and incorporate the best scientific and philosophic knowledge available. But religion itself seems to be primarily a way of feeling and acting, not a way of understanding and explaining. The relations of theology to explanation are much closer, so close that any theological formulation will inevitably reflect the knowledge of the society in which it is effected and will be strongly colored by the prevailing intellectual methods. But if we consider how even the theoretical beliefs of theology actually function in the religious life, it is difficult to see how they could seriously conflict with any scientific explanation.

The third position, then, assumes that all religious beliefs are mythology, and perform the essential religious functions of mythology, even should they incidentally turn out to be scientifically validated. They can perform these religious functions just as well if, taken literally, they are scientifically false; and they perform them no better if they can be proved, as men have tried to do again and again, to be scientifically true. That is, religious beliefs are "symbols," not expressions of knowledge but tools or instruments to be employed in the practice of religion.

These three positions are all widely maintained today. Catholics are officially committed to a combination of the first and the second, consecrated by Thomas Aquinas: they believe in both natural and revealed theology. Reflective Protestants by and large now hold to the second; during the eighteenth and nineteenth centuries they have had a vivid experience of the dangerous potentialities of the first, and have come to distrust all natural or "rational" theology. Many philosophers of religion coming from a Protestant background, however, are now tending to adopt the third position. I shall only say at this point that my own reflection has led me to adopt what is fundamentally a form of the third position: that, in the generally accepted sense, there is no "truth" at all in religion. Religious beliefs, though far indeed from being "meaningless," do not possess what is ordinarily meant by cognitive value.

But to rest with this flat denial would be misleading. Nor would the bald statement be completely accurate, or indeed even adequate practically. For these tentative conclusions depend on an analysis of the complex functioning of religious symbols, among which religious beliefs are central. And such inquiry must lead a candid mind to recognize essential values in both the first and the second positions that cannot be cavalierly disregarded. The first position is today in undeserved disrepute, especially among Protestants. Against its present detractors I want to say a word in behalf of rational or philosophical theology. As history makes clear, to reduce religious beliefs and symbols to the compass of any philosophic formulation, however well established, is tragic, and indeed, in the end, fatal. But this caution hardly leaves the enterprise of rational theology wholly invalid and without religious function. And though their claims are often confused and usually far from clear, the advocates of the second position are not entirely unjustified. Though religious beliefs are not symbols "of" any truths that could be stated literally, in non-symbolic language, there is a sense in which religious symbols are instruments of what can be said to be "revelation": for they can provoke religious vision, and they teach a kind of religious know-how.

It is on just the sense in which the third position needs qualification, to take account of the claims of the first and second when properly interpreted, that the consideration of religious symbols proves most illuminating. If the present analysis of religious knowledge seem in the end to give back what is at the outset taken away, there are philosophies today which could justify it as a "dialectical" treatment of religious "truth." But it is better to point to the obvious fact that the roles of knowledge in the enterprise of religion are actually manifold and complex, and call for careful and precise delimitation. It does not take much reflection on the problems to realize that any simple answer, like the exclusive adherence to one of the three positions, is bound to be inadequate. That is why we need all the illumination we can get from the long experience of religious history in our intellectually-minded culture.

Chapter One. *Religion and Greek Philosophy*

We Westerners hardly realize how distinctively Christian and indeed Protestant have been the problems presented by the intimate relations between knowledge and faith in our own religious tradition. No other culture has assigned so central a place to religious beliefs, and in no other has the refinement and criticism of primitive religious practices been so concerned with knowledge and understanding. Elsewhere the working over of religious materials has normally been moral and imaginative or artistic, not intellectual. Outside our Western tradition, the appearance of a philosophic or scientific interest has hardly provoked a rivalry with religion. All religions are rich in myth and legend. In the absence of any other ways of understanding the world, these are accepted without serious question. This imaginative lore has normally not been taken as "correct" or binding doctrine, but rather as something to be enjoyed and used, as the religious teacher uses parables, to point a moral or symbolize an ideal.

But characteristically, Christianity has always seen itself as a faith, and despite both Jesus and Paul faith soon came to mean correct or orthodox beliefs about God and man and human destiny. In sharp contrast, for both Judaism and Islam, religion has never been a faith to be believed, but rather a law to be followed. For Buddhism and Hinduism, it has been a way or a path of life to be pursued; for Confucianism, a code or standard of conduct to be observed. The Oriental religions have indeed been very practical, concentrating on conduct and behavior. They all take religion, not as a set of beliefs to be accepted as theoretically true, that could either learn from or come into serious competition with a secular philosophy or with science, but as a life to be lived, a path to be trodden. When confronted with new knowledge, and, more recently, with Western science, they have often indeed

15

found the novel ideas psychologically incompatible with their traditional lore. But they have rarely felt that intensity either of attraction or of logical contradiction that has been normal in Christianity. For them it has been new customs, not new ideas, that have proved disruptive.

In contrast with nearly every other religion, ever since the Christian gospel early in its career in the Hellenistic world began to appeal to men who had come under the influence of Greek philosophizing and developed a strong intellectual interest, Christianity has had a marked concern with explanation, with systematizing and organizing its beliefs into a "theology." And when Western Christianity rediscovered Greek philosophy in the Middle Ages, this concern with theological beliefs was intensified in the Schoolmen and their universities. It reached its height in the great Protestant reformers, who worked out subtle, elaborate, and profound systems of beliefs that expressed their deepest understanding of the world and of man. Just because they were rejecting what seemed to them corrupted doctrine, they insisted that to be saved all Christians must hold the correct or orthodox beliefs. They handed on this theological concern of theirs to later generations of Protestants. Partly because they were minimizing external observances and ritual, and partly because they were giving religious expression to a society in which the intellectual urge to understand was very strong, the heirs of the Reformation have traditionally assigned a central place to religious beliefs and to adequate intellectual interpretations.

But whatever the causes of this distinctive emphasis, it seems clear that religious beliefs and theology have never played the central role in most other religions that they have performed in Christianity in general and until recently in Protestantism in particular. In now at last minimizing theological formulations, in subordinating and forgetting the elaborate doctrinal systems which earlier distinguished the historic Protestant churches, in insisting that what a man believes does not count so long as he leads a Christian life, Americans seem in fact to have returned once more today to the more normal religious emphasis. There is a sound instinct in this distrust of intellectual difference in religion. In ceasing to be true to their historic Protestant past, American Protestants have actually become truer to the great tradition of religion. Even the recent efforts of the professionals to return to "Reformation theology" hardly alter these facts. For the "return" that is urged is not to a set of orthodox beliefs, but to a set of values that have once more become significant in our Age of Anxiety. The "Neo-Orthodox" are in fact less "orthodox" and more heretical than the Liberals: for they have abandoned the search for true doctrine in favor of more adequate symbols.

For the first fifteen hundred years of Christian history, the body of systematic thought most intimately related to religious knowledge was Greek philosophy. During all this time nothing we should recognize as "natural science" seemed to possess any special relevance for Christian faith. In the two centuries preceding the Christian era the Greeks had indeed built up a mathematical astronomy and physics that, when rediscovered in the thirteenth century, were developed directly into the scientific enterprise of the modern period. And medicine and biology, to say nothing of the glory of Greek scientific thought, mathematics, had already a history over twice as long. But this body of scientific ideas seemed neither to illuminate the Christian gospel, nor in any significant sense to compete with it. At no point did it touch upon the central Christian problems of salvation, of the relation of man to God, or the bitter questions of good and evil, of sin and grace. It was completely irrelevant to any religious knowledge.

With Greek philosophy, however, the case was entirely different. Here was a body of well-worked-out thought dealing with precisely these problems. Over a millennium of recorded experience had given this gifted people a store of human wisdom that still today seems unsurpassed. Some six centuries of patient analysis and speculative hypothesis by the most brilliant minds of antiquity, plumbing the profundities of the moral life and formulating its difficulties in intellectual terms, had carried the reflective consideration of how men can best live in their world as far as the unaided wit of man has ever been able to go. The Greek thinkers had developed a passion for understanding; they treated these problems in terms of knowledge—knowledge of the Good Life and how to attain it, knowledge of what is deathless and eternal in human nature, knowledge of the relations of both to the nature of things. They strove to work out an intelligible and logically consistent truth about the place of man in the cosmos, and about human destiny. Even frustration, failure, and ultimate doom the Greeks had to understand: tragedy was the most transparent intellectual vision of what man is and why he has to be so.

It was no accident that Greek philosophy was fundamentally concerned with moral and religious problems. It had come to birth when men began to reflect on the religious materials of their cultural heritage—feelings, practices, and ideas originally little different from those of the other and older Near Eastern civilizations. *Timor Dei principium sapientiae* was as true of Greek as of Hebrew wisdom. The earliest Greek cosmologies were rationalizations of the great creation myths of the Mesopotamian cultures. And the first philosophic ideas of the Greeks, which one succession of thinkers developed into scientific concepts, were the unquestioned assumptions they found in their religious tradition when they penetrated beneath the symbolic and imaginative forms with which the poets and artists had made vivid and human the surface.

The very success of Greek imagination in giving concrete and civilized embodiment to shadowy and fearful natural powers originally conceived with the same grotesque horror common to all the eastern Mediterranean religions, made it clear to the reflective that these forms must be the product of human art; the substance lay beneath. The efforts of the tragic poets to effect a moral reformation, to play the counterpart of the Hebrew prophets in refining moral standards, indeed failed religiously: the conduct quite appropriate for a natural principle of fertility was revolting in an anthropomorphized Zeus. But the very realization that the gods were now to be judged by human ethical standards reinforced the deep-seated conviction enshrined in the Olympian tradition, that morality was a human and social enterprise, a product of the *polis*, that it was the worst of sins, *hybris*, to seek to emulate the gods. Belief in the official political deities faded. They were left as a set of imaginative symbols, a projection of men's ideals and values, a cherished bond of union between the Hellenes, a common realm of the imagination for Greeks to dwell in and use. But the Good and the Divine were to be sought elsewhere. And they were to be found not in tradition but in reason and in knowledge.

Prevailingly hostile to the official Olympian religion, the philosophers found much more they could use in the other major strain in the Greek heritage, the tradition of the Mysteries and of Dionysos. Starting like the other mysteries or sacramental cults of Asia and Egypt in a fertility ritual, the Greek mysteries came to emphasize the Divine force and power not in Nature but in the group itself, in the group *daimon*, the living Dionysos, in whom his worshipers could participate, and thus gain a deathless and eternal life. At the hands of the intellectual Greeks they also came to emphasize a body of doctrine revealed to the initiates. Successive reformations by the Orphics and the Pythagoreans made these beliefs more scientific and even mathematical: it is in the presence of disinterested truth that the soul of man puts on deathlessness. With Orphics like Empedocles, and above all with the Pythagoreans, is to be found the first reconciliation of religion and science, the first identification of the object of religious feeling and aspiration with scientific truth.

This is the background of the Platonism of Plato: these are the religious symbols he drew upon to express and develop that philosophical theology, that rational doctrine of the Divine, in terms of which Christian theology was later worked out and formulated. For Plato was reacting against the extreme view of some of the Sophists, that moral standards are a purely human contrivance, the product of the political arts of the *polis*, of law or convention. He insisted that the Good and the Just are not human inventions, but human discoveries: the Good Life is grounded in the very nature of things. At the heart of the cosmos is a rational and intelligible structure—if we may believe Aristotle, like the Pythagoreans Plato thought it was mathematical in character—and what is Just and Good is to be discovered from the knowledge of this cosmic order. This intelligible realm of Ideas or rational order later came to be called the "Logos," or Objective Reason, and figured prominently not only in Neoplatonism but also in the philosophical theology of the Christians.

The other major Greek philosophy in the world in which the Christian gospel was proclaimed was Stoicism. Like the popular Platonism of the first century, it too grounded the moral life in the nature of things. It too found the rational nature of man intimately bound up with the rational "Nature" of the cosmos. It too founded its doctrine of man, its philosophical anthropology, upon its doctrine of the Divine, its rational theology. It differed from Platonism, as both differed from the Christian solution, in the relation it conceived to obtain between the Logos, the intelligible "Nature" of the cosmos, and the whole of things. For the Stoics, the Logos or Nature was immanent in the cosmos; for the Platonists, the Logos or Realm of Ideas transcended Nature and ordinary sense-experience. And the Stoics conceived this Reason in terms of a Moral Law rather than of the perfectings of human life discerned in imaginative vision—the Platonic Ideas. But the two philosophies were close enough to be easily blended in popular thought. And both had answers for all the religious problems for which the Christian gospel claimed to have the solution.

Above all, both these Greek philosophies alive in the first century made knowledge central—knowledge of man, knowledge of the Good, knowledge of the moral Nature of the cosmos, of the Divine. These were all important truths to be discovered. And though they were not an invention but a discovery, they were a human discovery. They were a discovery made by the reason of man, the deathless and eternal element in man which united him to the Divine. Socrates had conceived the quest for the Good Life as a search for something like the technical skill, the know-

how of the humble craftsman, the cobbler, the carpenter, or the
weaver. For Plato, it was rather a rational science of the Good,
like the mathematics which was the chief achievement of Greek
reason. In reaction, Aristotle thought of an intelligent art of diag-
nosis and healing, like that of the physician producing the health
of the soul. The Stoics proclaimed the rational Law of Good and
Right by which the universe is run. But whether craft, science,
art, or law, it was knowledge that was to be sought and cherished.
And it was to be found by man's reason, his logos, the human
power of understanding. Knowledge of the Good alone was not,
to be sure, enough: only Socrates seems to have held that true
knowledge is in itself virtue and moral excellence, and there is
doubt even about him. For Plato, there was needed also *eros,*
"love"; for Aristotle, the moral training that would produce the
habit of acting intelligently as a kind of second nature; for the
Stoics, the sternest kind of rational self-discipline. But knowledge
—of man's true Good, of its conditions in man's nature, and of
its grounding in the Divine Reason in the cosmos—was a necessary condition of the Good Life.

Such was the moral and religious wisdom offered by classic
Greek philosophy. But by the last century B.C. philosophy had
come even closer to the intellectual problems presented by the
Christian gospel. A revolution was taking place in men's moral
and religious experience, in which the confidence in man's natural
reason to discover the true Good and in man's natural moral
power to attain it measurably was giving way to a very different
attitude, a temper of humility, of self-abnegation, of impotence
and despair. Perhaps it would be more accurate to say that under
the sway of Rome free scope was given to the spread throughout
the Empire of religions from those Oriental lands which had never
felt the Greek sense of the power and the dignity of man, religions
expressing this temper of self-mistrust and despair of all human
efforts at deliverance. God must be pure and good and remote
from the evils of existence, so remote that he seemed quite inaccessible to all human efforts of intellect or will. Only the Divine

itself could bring saving knowledge and power to man. A host of incarnation and mystery cults appeared, in which the supreme and holy God of the universe sent his Son, or a Messenger, to live among men, to die for men, and to rise again, so that men, by sacramental union with this Lord of the cult, could secure the needful knowledge and power and rise with him. There was felt an intense need for a Mediator between the remote Divine and man, who by bringing the Divine into human life, could in turn bring man to God.

Philosophy became the rational expression of this kind of religious experience, and proceeded to make central the intellectual problems it posed. Even the confident Stoicism began to emphasize the moral struggle in the soul, springing from the conflict between reason and the Platonic irrational element it now took over; in Seneca it became an open confession of impotence and lack of power. The popular Platonism, whose religious inspiration had indeed started with the earlier Greek mysteries, became frankly the rationalization of this need for a Mediator. The philosophic problem now presented was how to reconcile a strong ethical dualism—the gulf between a Good that must be pure and the spotted actuality of human life—and an ultimate metaphysical monism; this Good must be the Supreme and All-controlling Reality. Before it could accept any of the proposed Mediators—the deputy gods and *daimons* of Plutarch, the number-messengers or angels of the Neo-Pythagoreans, the Lords of any of the mystery cults, or Jesus the Christ, the Son of God—the Greek mind still had to understand. The Truth that sets men free from sin and death might turn out to be not a discovery of human knowledge and reason, but a self-revelation of the Divine itself. But men still had to "believe" it, and to grasp intellectually how salvation could take place.

It was Philo Judaeus, intellectual leader of the great colony of Hellenized Jews in Alexandria, who harmonized this religious philosophy with the Hebraic tradition, and in so doing became the father of Christian exegesis, and the formulator of the main lines

of Christian theology. His method was the allegorical interpretation of the Scriptural Law, in which he identified the imaginative
symbols of Hebrew poetry and prophesy with the rational concepts
of Greek thought. He was the first to make the Logos a Mediator
between God and man. In Platonism, the objective Intelligible
Structure, taken as the highest "realm" in the cosmos, was the
Divine itself; in Stoicism the intelligible Logos was likewise God,
though conceived as wholly immanent in the universe. For Philo,
the Logos was God's Agent in Creation, the sum of God's powers,
those various Powers the Scriptures symbolize as "Angels" or
Messengers, and above all God's Power and Wisdom, known to
Holy Writ as Seraphim and Cherubim. The Logos was "divine,"
theos, and was embodied in the Law and in the High Priest. The
Logos was to be distinguished from the "Eternal One," "God,"
ho theos, primarily in worship. The Logos was to be worshiped
by the observance of the Law, while the Eternal was to be worshiped freely in faith.

In Philo the Jew we can already see how Greek knowledge
was to enter into the later Christian faith. On the one hand, it
furnished a philosophical interpretation of the religious symbols
and the mythical images of the religious tradition. It enabled Philo
to understand, in terms of the best thought available in his day,
ideas which, had he been forced to construe them literally, he
would have had to reject as false. It made it possible for him to
appreciate and retain the religious and moral insight concealed in
traditional legend and prophetic vision. This interpretation introduced intellectual consistency into the thought of a cultivated
man anxious to hold to the Hebraic tradition while also welcom-
ing the wisdom of Greek thought. This avoidance of contradiction
between religious beliefs and explanatory ideas is, to be sure, an
intellectual rather than a religious value, and in so far Philo's
philosophical theology serves a logical rather than a religious function. But surely to give religious consecration to intellectual values,
to include truth in the object of worship, is a genuine and essential
religious value. And to make it possible to recognize religious

insight underneath imaginative form is to perform a religious function. Intellectual reinterpretation is a necessary part of religious faith—for the intellectual.

On the other hand, Greek knowledge brought Philo at many points into conflict with his Hebrew predecessors. He followed the Platonists in exalting the Divine so high above human life that he had to deny to it any of the attributes encountered in human experience, including those traits found in man's relations with his fellows that are so important a part of the imagery of worship and prayer. He is one of the pioneers of "negative theology," convinced that only the contradictory of every finite quality can be applied to God. Hence he had to employ an often strained allegorical interpretation of the Scriptures to get rid of every anthropomorphic characteristic in the Divine, even the notion of "Father," of personality itself. The least inadequate symbol of the Divine, he held, is the human mind contemplating impersonal truth.

Finally, Philo remained an orthodox Jew: he held strictly to the observance of the Law. His Greek way of understanding in no wise interfered with his actual practice of the religious life. Rather, it strengthened it immeasurably. Nor did he try to substitute knowledge for faith. Philo is the great philosopher of faith. He is as much suffused by it as Paul, and in a similar mystical sense. Not in knowledge but in faith must we worship and serve the Eternal. But faith for Philo was a religious commitment, not a higher form of knowledge. In his religion he remained a Hebrew, but in his way of understanding that religion he was a Greek. Contemporary with the birth of the Christian gospel, he is a cardinal illustration of how one may give a fresh intellectual interpretation to the traditional symbols of a living religious faith, while still using those symbols in the practice of the religious life.

The early Jewish Christians remained Jews, with no thought of a new religion; they were convinced that Jesus was the Messiah or "Christ," and they regarded his Messiahship as much more important than his moral message. That is, they believed *in* Jesus, rather than *that* what Jesus taught was true—an attitude that marks most Christian thought until the nineteenth century. This conviction involved certain intellectual beliefs or expectations: that only righteous, Law-observing Jews who accepted Jesus as the Messiah would share in the Kingdom he would set up on his second coming. But their faith in Jesus was primarily a commitment to Jesus: it was practical rather than intellectual.

Much the same holds true of Paul, though his conception of the work of the Christ was quite different: not to found the Kingdom, but to transform human nature from flesh to spirit, and thus save individual persons from bondage to sin and death. By accepting and "believing in" the Christ men are united to him in a mystical union, die with him, put off the flesh with him, and rise with him, completely transformed in nature, to a new and divine life in the spirit, a life "in Christ." This is for Paul all an intensely personal and practical religious experience. "Believing in" Christ is much more than a commitment, it is a complete union. And "faith" is no mere intellectual assent and acceptance; it is utter absorption.

Yet Paul was a Hellenized Jew who had to understand. The whole framework of the redemptive system, in terms of which he interpreted the salvation he had won on the road to Damascus, is paralleled in, if not actually borrowed from, the many mystery cults of the time, with their widespread myth of a dying and rising Savior and Lord. He had to construe his own bitter and joyful experience in intelligible terms. Why? How? Why could he not keep the Law? Who and what was the living and divine Christ who had saved him? What was the character of his supernatural life "in Christ" and the spirit after he had risen with Christ? To answer these questions he had to work out a whole theology. To the many inquiries of his fellow Christians he was never at a loss for an answer—"God forbid!"

This well-rounded body of ideas that is Paul's theology is an instance of the primary function of knowledge in the religious life: to interpret that life intellectually, to answer the questions raised directly by what has happened in one's own religious experience. Paul was doubtless mistaken in universalizing his individual travail and rebirth. But Paul never mistook the theology that explained his living experience for a way of salvation, or set its acceptance as a condition of redemption. The later Church did so treat some of Paul's ideas, and with the Protestants his whole theology was made essential: was it not to be found in the Scriptures? What Paul preached was Christ crucified, and the promise of release from sin and death through union with him: what he had learned at first hand. He had little interest in Jesus of Nazareth or his "teachings"; they were not what had saved him, but the living and risen Christ. Is it any wonder that his questions, and his theological answers, were about the Living Christ, not about the teachings of Jesus?

The author of the Fourth Gospel—conventionally "John"—while sharing Paul's conception of Christianity as a redemptive system, has interests that are much more philosophical and intellectual. He is the first to bring Greek thought to the interpretation of the Christian universe, adopting in his prologue Philo's Logos. For him the transformation of human nature effected by union with Christ is an intellectual illumination, a change from a "realm of darkness" to a "realm of light"—perhaps, if recent evidence may be believed, a continuation of the teachings of the Essenes. For him, Jesus is a teacher, who came to show God to men: "This is Life Eternal, that they shall know thee the only true God." He wrote a gospel—Paul was characteristically not interested—to make clear Jesus's vision of God as Love. Union with Christ comes through "faith," which "John" takes intellectually as belief, and hence must occur also through "love." The two had been fused in Paul. For Paul, "faith" is a mystic activity; for "John," it is much more Greek, a spirit of receptivity toward the vision shown by Christ. With the Fourth Gospel, a "higher" form of knowledge, the true revelation of God, becomes central in Christianity.

This "higher" knowledge was elaborated by the Gnostics, the

most speculative Christian thinkers of the second century. This religious gnosis necessary to salvation involved an elaborate cosmology derived from Persian sources, and was exclusive and aristocratic: hence only the intellectual elite could hope to be saved. But the Gnostics repelled most Christians by their extreme dualism, their bitter anti-Judaism, their denial of Providence and the Incarnation. They provoked a marked reaction. On the one hand, it was the Gnostics who were responsible for the first Christian creed, the Apostles' Creed, which was formulated in Rome about 150 A.D.: candidates for baptism had to declare their intellectual disagreement with the Gnostics, especially with Marcion, and their adherence to the teachings of the Apostles. Thus doctrinal standards were for the first time made a necessary condition for salvation. On the other hand, the Christian philosophy of the Alexandrian Doctors arose as the intellectual answer to the errors of the Gnostics.

Besides this mystical interpretation, which saw Christianity as a redemptive system for the transformation of human nature, appealing to few Christians at first, but growing rapidly in the second century, until it was discredited by the Gnostics, there was a moral interpretation, far more popular, especially among Jewish and Roman Christians. This saw Christianity as a kind of universalized Judaism, a revealed law of conduct and a promise of immortality, an ethical code with religious sanctions, with no nonsense about supernatural redemption about it. This interpretation appealed to many of the popular Stoic preachers or "philosophers," who on conversion not unnaturally viewed Christianity as the true philosophy. Correct knowledge of the true God is the essence of philosophy, and Christianity has it. These men, all "philosophers" or liberal preachers by profession, undertook to explain the meaning of Christianity to the Hellenistic world. For Greek thinkers, they became the first rationalizers and intellectual justifiers of the Christian revelation.

Justin Martyr is just such a typical second century Apologist. He emphasizes the three tenets of later "rational religion": there is an omnipotent God, he has commanded a law of righteousness, and he will punish and reward men in a future life. Man is a free being, but stupid and forgetful. He needs to be reminded of these truths that he could reach by his natural reason. Christ came, not to bring magic grace, not to give any new teaching, but to repeat to men that God meant what he said. Christ merely reaffirmed the true philosophy of Heraclitus, Socrates, and Plato, who were all Christians because they were right. The Logos, the supreme Reason, who inspires men with all their human reason and truth, inspired the Prophets, and became incarnate in Christ, who as a teacher made things a little clearer and more certain, and renewed the revelation of the eternal Divine Law. Other Apologists lost the sense of anything distinctive in Christianity; it was merely true philosophy and rational religion. "All Christianity is in the first six chapters of Genesis." Theophilus, for instance, never mentions Christ at all. For the Apologists, the Christian revelation was knowledge, and a knowledge competely identified with secular philosophy.

Two major intellectual developments took place in the ancient Church. With real philosophical interests, the Alexandrian Neo-platonic theologians, Clement of Alexandria, Origen, Gregory Thaumaturgos, and Athanasius, worked out the doctrines of the Trinity and of the Person of Christ, defending Greek values and conceptions against the Syrian ascetics and dualists of the School of Antioch. Orthodox doctrine was determined in the oecumenical councils, especially those of Nicaea and Chalcedon; the decisions, though political compromises, like those among dialectical materialists in Russia today, forever enshrined Platonism and the Platonic philosophy at the intellectual heart of the Christian tradition. The other great doctrinal achievement of the ancient Church was the intellectual formulation of the cardinal Roman experience of sin and salvation, by grace through the Church, worked out by the great Latin Fathers, Cyprian, Ambrose, and Augustine. The two bodies of ideas were united by Augustine, who was philosophically half Greek and half Roman.

The doctrines of the Trinity and of the Incarnation were worked out in the Eastern or Greek Church. They are the first great instance of the identification of Christian truth with rational knowledge, the first "rational" or "natural" theology, the first systematic interpretation of the Christian symbols in terms of a speculative and philosophical theology. In contrast to the theology of Paul, which was an effort to understand a personal living experience, they are the attempt to come to terms with a well-worked-out and established philosophical system, the Neoplatonic philosophy. In the Latin Church, the Trinity has normally been taken as a mystery of faith, not intelligible to human reason. It was there accepted first on the authority of the Nicene Council, not because it was understood, or seemed to explain anything, but as a sign of submission to the authority of the Church. Later attempts to "explain" the Trinity in terms of other philosophies have always proved to lead to heresy. Hence in the West the tradition has grown up that the Trinity is not to be explained. For the Greeks, in contrast, the Trinity was originally not a mystery, but a rational and philosophical explanation.

This is characteristic of the great contrast in developed Christian philosophy between the Eastern and Western Churches in ancient times. The Latin Church was interested in a way of life, in moral problems. Its concerns were the practical conditions of the moral life: sin, salvation, grace, and the Church. For the Romans, life was serious, a pretty solemn affair. It was so hard to do right! They were pessimists, and they welcomed "Oriental" thought: it expressed their values. They loved authority in both Empire and Church; they were enthusiastic for the magic transformation of human nature, for dualism and asceticism. They had a Puritan conscience; they were natural born deacons and moral reformers. They were willing to do anything but think. They hated Greek naturalism and reasonableness. They built their theology on Paul and his Oriental dualism and magic, and his rigoristic moralism.

In contrast, the ancient Greek Church was intellectual, and interested in speculative problems. Its thinkers felt the need to understand the universe, to live naturally and rationally. They could not accept any religious or theological doctrine they did not understand. And they passed on naturally to philosophical inquiry for its own sake, even if its bearing on salvation were not immediately apparent. Christianity presented the Greek theologians with intellectual problems. They had to solve them in the world of Greek philosophy, and express them in its language, just as we have to express and solve our intellectual problems in the world and the language of evolutionary and experimental science. The Romans hated science and culture: they were Fundamentalists. The Greeks were not Fundamentalists: they were something that is perhaps rather worse, intellectuals. Fortunately, Augustine was himself half Greek, or he would have transmitted to the Western tradition far less in the way of intellectual materials. One trembles to think of the consequences had Tertullian been the great Latin Father.

The Alexandrian Platonic theologians were typical religious liberals. They were intelligent, cultivated men, opposed to Oriental irrationalism and pessimism. They were broad-minded, tolerant, eclectic, imaginative and not literal-minded. They were rationalistic and naturalistic in their devotion to typically Greek values. They worked out a rounded philosophical theology and Christology, in the language of the prevalent Hellenistic religious philosophies, that expressed their interpretation of the Christian insight in terms of those values and attitudes. The terms of the Trinitarian doctrine—the "Father," the "Logos" or "Word," the "Spirit"—were traditional Christian symbols, embodied in the ancient baptismal formula. But the signification given them, and the relations established between them by the Alexandrians, were essentially philosophical. For the Alexandrians, the Trinity and the discussions leading up to its formulation were far from an incomprehensible mystery of faith. They were an intelligible answer to intellectual problems, a philosophical solution, not a perplexing enigma.[1]

Alexandrian thought is indeed very hard for us moderns to understand; for it is couched in terms of the Platonic philosophy of "substances" and their relations. Our own all-embracing scientific order of nature, and the general philosophical monism as to substance prevailing since the end of the eighteenth century, make us think in terms not of the relations between different "substances," but of different functions within the same "substance" —of activities, behaviors, means, ends, and values. The Platonists thought of distinctions and relations between separate "substances." For us, there is only one nature, one reality, one substance; we make our distinctions within that single nature in terms of different operations and values. The Platonists, in other words, talked in terms of nouns and adjectives, while we use verbs and adverbs. To understand what the Trinity meant to the Platonists, we must never forget these two quite different philosophical languages.

Take the question of the relation between God, conceived as one "substance," and the world, another "substance." The problem is an intensely vital one today: the issue is, in our language, "Can we hope to realize our ideals, to attain our ends? How far can we expect to achieve our values?" It is the issue between op-

[1] Of course, the Alexandrian Christian Platonists, being typical religious liberals, failed to achieve complete philosophical clarity in their reinterpretations of the traditional scriptural symbols. Above all, they did not aim to state explicitly just what they were rejecting. Like all mediators, they emphasized the positive values and attitudes they felt to be important. They would doubtless have been hard put to it themselves to define precisely the negative implications of their thought. And it is still a debated question how far the Platonic language they were employing is itself a symbolic rendering of human experience. But Clement of Alexandria, in defending the true "Christian gnostic" against the false "Oriental" or Marcionite Gnostic, is clear enough about the values he is maintaining. And so is Origen, though his language and the terms for his principles are definitely personal and Catholic.

In the following interpretation of the doctrine of the Trinity as a "rational theology," the emphasis is on these human values expressed, not on the extent to which either the traditional scriptural language or that of philosophic Platonism was itself recognized to be symbolic.

timism and pessimism, between progress and decay, between meliorism and cynicism, between a pragmatic attitude and Communist absolutism.

Or take the Logos, which involved for the Greeks the whole problem of science and knowledge. The Platonists asked, "Is there a 'rational substance,' a 'reason' or Logos, in the universe? Is it identical with the highest 'substance,' or does the highest 'substance' lie above it, and remain inaccessible to it, so that reality transcends and eludes the intellectual grasp of knowledge, and we must fall back on a nonrational revelation?" In our different fashion, we ask: "How far can we hope to achieve knowledge? Do the most important truths of all transcend all human knowledge? How ultimate is our science? How far is it 'mere'?"

Or take the Holy Spirit, which as a "substance" meant man's natural moral power and good will. Is it adequate to meet the problems of living, or do we need a supernatural grace to transform man's "substance"? The relation between the Logos and the Holy Spirit is the relation between intelligence and moral power. Are they ultimately identical, or are they wholly disparate? This is the issue between a liberalism which trusts to man's intelligence, and a revolutionary radicalism which trusts the economic process, and ultimately falls back on force.

Or consider the divinity of Christ. The Platonists conceived it in terms of the attributes of his "substance"; we, in terms of what he did. The Platonists ask the nature of Christ's "substance"; we ask the value of his functioning. The Platonists said, Christ's "substance" is divine; we say, Christ's life and teaching are of supreme value—the ideal of Love symbolized in Christ is divine. The Virgin Birth is hence for the Platonist a natural myth or symbol; for the evolutionary naturalist, it is highly inappropriate and meaningless. Thus, if a secular analogy may be pardoned, the Platonist might well ask, "Was the United Nations 'born of a virgin'?" and might well go on then naturally to the "immaculate conception" of Franklin Roosevelt. We of course would put it, "How great is the value of the United Nations? What good can it accomplish?" We are not particularly interested in Roosevelt's "substance," and the expression is very alien; but it is clearly the same issue.

We find it hard even to understand the idea of God as "Being" —our muddled theists seem often all mixed up. What the Platonists called *theios,* "Divine," we call our ideals, our controlling values, our "ultimate concern"—but we mean the same thing.

Consider the problems of the Alexandrians. Is man corrupt and fallen in "substance," or is he free, made in God's image? This is the issue between Augustine and the Latin Fathers on the one hand, and Clement and Origen and the Greeks on the other. It means, "Is the Good Life to be a thing of restrictions and repressions, or a natural development guided by intelligence?" The view of Augustine leads to the Eighteenth Amendment and the censorship of plays; the view of Clement leads to temperance and a free stage.

Is God "transcendent" or "immanent," far-off or indwelling? This is the issue between the Arians and Tertullian, and Clement, Origen, and Athanasius. It means, "Is the Good Life impossibly beyond man, or is it within man's power? Is it something externally imposed, or is it the wise use of natural impulses? Are science, art, and civilization bad, and to be rejected, or are they good, and to be furthered? Is man to be viewed as full of the old Adam, or as potentially divine? Is it all a bad business, or can we hope and work for a better world?"

This is all summed up in the doctrine of the Trinity. Is the Christ-Logos "very God of very God, begotten, not made, of one substance with the Father"? The formula means nothing in our lives, and is as devoid of intellectual import to the man reciting it today, as it is irrelevant to those who have never heard of it. Is the Logos of the "same substance" with the Father, or only of "like substance"? Is it *homoousios,* or only *homoiousios*? The difference, being a single iota, is always good for a laugh today. But to the Christian Platonist the issue was not silly. The Trinity, in its doctrine of the relations of "substances," summed up the fundamental contentions of his religious philosophy. It meant the victory of Greek rationalism and humanism over Oriental asceticism and irrational faith. It meant that the Good Life, founded on knowledge, and sustained by the natural moral power of the Christian brotherhood, is possible and attainable. "Natural reason," or knowledge in the world, the principle of Christ, the Logos, the inspiration of all human science and wisdom, is the highest good, the only valid human ideal. It is not subordinate to anything else; there is nothing above it, eluding its grasp. It is the supreme "substance." The "natural moral power" of men, the Pneuma or "Holy Spirit" indwelling them, especially the Christian community, is sufficient for men's needs. There is no necessity of magic or miracle, of a transformation of human nature.

The Incarnation means that Jesus of Nazareth, in his character, acts, and teaching of Love for God and for one's neighbor, is the highest moral excellence, or fully *theios,* "Divine." Moreover, the incarnation of the Logos in Jesus was not a unique miracle, but rather a particular instance of the universal incarnation of the Logos in all men. It was a revelation of man's "essential nature," of man's moral and intellectual possibilities, of his potential divinity. This was the view of Athanasius. The Greek Platonists said, God is "incarnate" in humanity. To express the same values, we should say, human nature, enlightened by reason and intelligence, and filled with good will, is "divine"—man can live the Good Life, with no need of asceticism or magic rites.

To Clement, Origen and Athanasius, the doctrine of the Trinity expressed their Greek humanism and naturalism; while the denial of the Trinity, Arianism, the subordination of the Logos, meant the denial of the validity of natural reason, natural moral power, and the natural life of man. Hence in modern terms, since the decisions of the Councils of Nicaea and Chalcedon have always determined Christian orthodoxy, the views of the so-called Neo-Orthodox are clearly heretical, a version of the Arian heresy; and every good Christian is naturally entitled to pronounce them anathema. Only a good Christian would have the authority to deliver such a curse—and anyway, it would hardly be merciful to do a thing like that to such good, if misguided, people. But as an historian, it is my clear duty to point out that the Neo-Orthodox do reject both the Trinity and the Incarnation, in their original meaning, and are hence hardly to be considered as Christians, though they may be pretty good Hebrew prophets.

Arius was an apostle of the Oriental thought of the School of Antioch. He stressed the immense gulf between the human and the Divine, between man and the Highest. He emphasized the arbitrary power and authority of God, and extreme asceticism. For Arius, the Logos is a Demiurge, an ambassador of God to man, revealing the impassable chasm between man and God, proclaiming the Divine Judgment on man, and exacting unquestioning obedience to his Divine Master. Hence Karl Barth is quite literally an Arian. Arius hated the rationalism and humanism of the Greek Fathers, their doctrine of the immanence of God; and he resolved to unite the Oriental bishops against it—all those who looked to the School of Antioch for leadership.

Athanasius, in contrast, was Greek in his thought and values. He grew up in the tradition of Alexandrian thought, for which God was not remote, but fills the world and mankind with his presence. The "Divine" in mankind, man's reason and moral will, the Logos and the Pneuma, are of the "same substance" with the Father, with the Highest, *homousios*. That one "substance" or *ousia* could be wholly in each "Person" or *Prosopon* of the Trinity, as well as in humanity, and in one man, Jesus, was of course a commonplace of the universally accepted Platonic logical realism, just as the whole essence of humanity could be in Adam, and in each man. This was no mystery to the Platonist!

Of course, the values which the Greek philosophical theologians expressed in their doctrine of the Trinity did not long continue to be what that doctrine came to symbolize in the Christian tradition, especially in the Latin Church, which understood neither those values nor the Platonic philosophy in which they were formulated.[2] But without a knowledge of the original meaning of the Trinity, it is impossible to understand how again and again Christian Platonists, like Augustine, and the long line of Augustinians, Bonaventura, Cusanus, Malebranche, Hegel, when they really grasped the meaning of the doctrines of the Trinity and the Incarnation, could find in them an admirable formulation of those humanistic and naturalistic ideals they had come to share.

I have dwelt on the Alexandrian doctrines of the Trinity and the Incarnation because they illustrate so admirably one of the characteristic roles of knowledge in the religious life. They are not, like the theology of Paul, the intellectual construing of a living experience. They are not fundamental religious beliefs—beliefs which function in the practice of the religious arts, like communion or prayer or worship. They are frankly speculative and philosophical, the answer to primarily intellectual rather than to primarily religious problems. Indeed, Origen, who largely formulated them, intended them for theologians interested in knowledge, not for Christians in general; he did not consider them necessary for salvation. For that, faith, *pistis,* is sufficient; it consists in the accepted teachings of the Church, embodied in the creed. After accepting these articles of faith, the intellectual Christian will then go on to knowledge; he will try to understand his faith. It was the accident of the Arian controversy, in which they came to symbolize the fundamental religious and moral values of the Alexandrian Neoplatonists, that led to their formulation as a shibboleth in the Nicene creed. And even then it was the smallest of the three parties at the Council of Nicaea that won out, Hosius the Alexandrian rewriting the compromising creed of Eusebius in Trinitarian terms. And the later interpretation of the Church, worked out by the Cappodocian Fathers, construed the Nicene formula in terms of the Semi-Arian position:

[2] We have already pointed out that the Greek theologians themselves used a "supernaturalistic" language to express their rational and human values, without bothering to go into how far that Platonic language was itself symbolic in character.

not Athanasius's "same being in three forms," but "three persons of the same 'nature.' "

Yet the Trinity remains the greatest and the most successful instance in the Christian tradition of a "rational" and, in the later sense, a "natural" theology. It is an intellectual interpretation of the meaning of symbols, which in their imaginative form are used in the concrete religious arts. It interprets them by means of the concepts of a philosophical system worked out to make intelligible the world as the scene of human experience. It uses Greek philosophy to understand the meaning of the Christian symbols, just as Philo had used it to understand the Jewish symbols. Its primary function is logical, in the interest of intellectual consistency. But it is more: like Philo's doctrine, it has a genuinely religious function, for those intellectuals who have understood their experience in the light of Neoplatonism.

Intellectuals can, and have, used many other later schemes of understanding to construe the Christian symbols, down to Whitehead in our own day. Rational or natural theology has an undying appeal, for it performs an essential function for intelligent men. But the experiments of history make clear that the scheme of understanding employed must be a scheme which illuminates man and his experience. The Trinity is the most successful of all rational theologies because Platonism managed to do just that. The only other really successful Christian natural theology, that of Thomas Aquinas, is not so adequate as the Platonic Trinity, because the Aristotelian science Thomas used was oriented more to nature than to man, and he employed primarily the Aristotelian physics. Had he drawn more on the *Ethics* and the *Politics,* the results might have been quite different. The natural theology of the eighteenth century failed miserably, because Newtonian science left the whole of human life unintelligible. The Trinity was so successful that it and its terms could themselves be transformed into genuinely religious symbols, and as such far outlast their original meaning as an intellectual solution to philosophical problems.

The Western or Latin Church exhibited the temper of the Romans: it had little interest in philosophy or theology, but great concern with political organization. Its major leaders have been not thinkers but statesmen—or politicians. Its supreme intellectual achievement, Scholasticism, is the organization of knowledge rather than its discovery, the adjustment of beliefs through intellectual statesmanship. Arnobius is typical of the ancient Latin Church: "What business is it of yours to inquire into nature, or into the origin of souls? Leave all knowledge and science to God. The salvation of souls is the only thing you are permitted to inquire about." All the heresies came from the questioning Greeks; in the West arose rather schisms, political revolts. The great task was to build the Church, that truly marvelous institution. The Greeks had no organized Church, a fact typical of their lack of interest in social organization. Hence the Eastern churches were easily dominated by the State, whereas in the West the Church soon became supreme.

The old Roman religion had been formal and political. It was founded on fear: the gods were very far from men. There was no trace of mysticism about it. Roman Christianity came as a new law: salvation is obedience to rightful authority. When the West achieved an independent philosophy, in Augustine, it made authority central: the vital question was man's disobedience to God and his obedience to the Church. The Good Life was regarded as utterly unnatural and irrational: without the fear of Hell, the most rational course would be to enjoy all the lusts of the flesh. This was the view stated by Lactantius and Ambrose. Sin was not ignorance but disobedience. Man needs not knowledge but submission to the Divine authority of the Church. Philosophy and doctrine coming from the East were accepted, not as knowledge or as explanations of intellectual problems, but as a sign of submission to constituted authority.

The Roman Christians, when they thought, thought as lawyers, in terms of legal concepts, with no mysticism. They dealt with relations, not between substances, but between legal personalities and wills, an attitude that naturally played havoc with the Trinity. Their philosophical concepts were Stoic. Neoplatonism did not reach the West until the fourth century, with Ambrose and Augustine, when the issues had been already formulated in legal and Stoic terms. It then presented to Roman thinkers the characteristic problems of adjusting divergent ideas.

Tertullian is typical. He was a lawyer, a good man, and a ranting Fundamentalist. A man of tender feeling, he shrank from all cruelty, sacrificed his career to join the Christians because he had to stand with the oppressed—and he preached a ruthless hell-fire gospel. God is a personal Sovereign, stern and just; he is good, but his wrath and hatred for the sinner are mighty. Above all, God is absolute power: "I would rather have a wicked God than a weak one." Man is God's subject, and owes him fear and humility: there can be no morality without fear. Man owes God unquestioning obedience. We are wicked if we obey God's law because it seems to us good; we must obey it as God's command. Do and believe what you are told. "To know nothing in opposition to the Rule of Faith is to know all things. . . . Remain in ignorance, lest you should know what you ought not to." Believe, because it is irrational and incredible, and therefore Divine. "It is certain, because it is impossible." Away with philosophy and natural reason! "What has Athens in common with Jerusalem? We need no curiosity after Jesus, and no inquiry after the Gospel." Believe because of the authority of tradition; there is no other rational truth. Faith is to be accepted as the property of the Church, owned by the right of prescription. The questioner is a thief and a robber. "Faith is my property—get off!" Never argue with a heretic, invoke the law. Tradition, possession, prescription is the final test of truth. It is clear that for Tertullian, as for most of the Latin Fathers, the role of knowledge in Christianity was not a central problem.

Yet Tertullian was a Stoic materialist, one of the few major Christian theologians to hold to materialism: only body is real. Hence God is corporeal, the soul, reason—grace is a bodily substance. Tertullian shows what Christianity was like without Platonism—or Paul! Salvation is escape from Hell; it is wholly legal in character. It is legal acquittal, being declared "just" at the Judgment Seat. Tertullian was a Puritan: revolted by the Church's acceptance of the world, he gave up everything a second time to join the rigorous sect of Montanists. He himself became a heretic. He stood for his principles, and was condemned by them: he was now the robber!

With Augustine, formulator of the whole body of wisdom of ancient Christianity and transmitter of the deposit of the faith to the West, we encounter a man of very different stamp. He is the greatest mind of the ancient Church, and clearly the most influential of all the philosophers in the Western tradition. He had two great advantages over his Latin colleagues. His vivid and varied personal experience gave all these different ideas a vital and personal meaning to him, so that his entire thought speaks with the sincerity of Paul's theology. And he knew Greek philosophy, and hence could not give up intelligence and reason, so that his speculative and rational theology became in the West the Christian form of the great Platonic tradition, Christian Platonism. Thus Augustine illustrates all the different roles which knowledge can play in the religious life. At the same time, he carried on the tradition of Philo, Clement and Origen, that Scripture and the religious arts deal in symbols which cannot be understood literally. Indeed, he did not accept Christianity until Ambrose assured him authoritatively that he need not take any of its symbolic beliefs in the first or literal sense, but only allegorically.

Augustine was a man converted to Christianity. Hence his whole rational theology is, like Paul's, a theology of conversion. The other great Christian rational theologian, Thomas Aquinas, was a man who was explaining his natural environment. Christianity could not possibly mean the same thing to two men of such different experience. The great nineteenth-century Romantic "Christian" rational theologies—those of Schleiermacher, Hegel,

Schelling, Kierkegaard, Ritschl—came from men converted from traditional Christianity to other views: to the "teachings of Jesus," to modern humanism, to Romantic *Weltschmerz,* to humanitarianism, social reform, and collectivism.

The convert feels deep needs, and has found something that answers them. That "something" is naturally so important for him that it overshadows everything else, and is inevitably set off by a sharp gulf from the rest of the world. There is the precious thing, and then there is all else: "supernaturalism" is a natural fact in the experience of the convert, the "finder." Now Augustine was a man of deep needs, and very diverse needs: he felt man's weakness in so many ways! He tasted many philosophies, looking for deliverance and strength, and he found something in them all. He was at first a Manichaean, because he felt the moral struggle between Good and Evil so keenly; Manichaeism was the fourth-century successor to Gnosticism and Persian dualism. He felt the need for moral and ethical salvation; and though he consciously broke with Manichaean tenets, he retained their main conviction, the eternal gulf between Good and Evil, and the unalterable election of the few to salvation and of the many to damnation. He remained an ethical dualist.

Augustine then became a Neoplatonist, because he felt the need of the mystic to sink into Supreme Reality. An intellectual and logical mystic, he saw all knowledge as dependent on and leading to the Supreme Truth or Reason, *Sapientia* or Wisdom. An ethical mystic, he saw all good as dependent on and leading to absolute Goodness, Supreme Being or Reality. Anything independent is less real, and therefore evil. Adherence to Supreme "Being" is the only good, the only life, and turning away is itself evil and death. Augustine's conception of knowledge, and his ontology of Being, remained fundamentally Neoplatonic: he is the logical mystic, the metaphysical monist. Finally, Augustine was a sceptic: man by himself is nothing, he has no truth, no power, no life, he is only a mass of needs. Hence he felt the appeal of authority, as the sceptic always does: he remained the

Churchman, the Bishop, the sacramentarian. Augustine was an empiricist who tested all things in the fire of his own burning experience, a rationalist with a Platonic vision of Truth all naked and alone, and an institutionalist who fully realized the human craving for social authority.

Augustine's final philosophical theology embodied all these experiences, and answered all these needs. Hence it is a weaving together, with marvelous subtlety, of different strains logically independent, and in most men psychologically incompatible. It is not suggested there are major "inconsistencies" in Augustine's thought. But the connections are to be found in his rich experiences, not in any unified dialectical system of ideas. He did formulate a rational theology making it all intelligible. In controversy, he was pushed away from Platonism to the dualistic, Manichaean, Oriental attitude; at the end he was near Mohammed.

This is not the place to set forth Augustine's great doctrines: his theory of knowledge and metaphysics of Being, his doctrine of sin and salvation through grace, his theory of the Church as a Divine institution and authority, his doctrine of the City of God, of Christian society and of the philosophy of history. His eager mind brought the best knowledge and thought of his day to bear on each of these problems: there was nothing he touched he did not illuminate. Even his most speculative theories, in which he pushed Platonism farthest, his theory of knowledge, his doctrine of the Trinity, his Neoplatonic explanation of evil as sheer nonbeing, were brought to the service of the Living God who had saved him. Central to each of them is that only real "Being." In Augustine there is the complete and perfect fusion between the knowledge of the thinker and the faith of the saint. Our own sanctity is more than dubious, and our knowledge far richer than the Platonism at Augustine's disposal. But what he accomplished in his time can stand as the ideal, the very Platonic Idea, of the role of knowledge in the religious life.

Chapter Two. *Religion and Natural Science*

We left Christianity in Augustine with a fully formulated rational or speculative theology. It now possessed a rounded intellectual interpretation of both its theoretical and practical problems, in terms of the accepted Platonic scheme of understanding of the Hellenistic culture in which it had come to maturity. The very success of this incorporation of the knowledge of the ancient world, the very completeness of this reconciliation between the Christian gospel and its intellectual environment, made inevitable a clash with any new scheme of understanding that might be developed. This was quite over and beyond the particular clash between the Hellenistic scheme of values it had come to embody and express so fully, and the values of the totally different kind of social experience of the new and alien Western culture that happened rather accidentally to take it over. On both these two counts, the civilization of Western Europe, which began to take organized form during the eleventh and twelfth centuries, came into conflict with the Christian scheme it had inherited and was just beginning to try to understand. Its social experience generated a set of moral values that at best seemed irrelevant to those of Augustinian Christianity, and at worst completely incompatible with them. In the service of these values it soon developed intellectual interests that led it to formulate successive bodies of natural science that came into sharp conflict with the Augustinian Platonism that had seemed the only possible intellectual interpretation of its religious faith.

The dominant force in Western civilization has been the steady increase in the scope and importance of its economic and technological activities. This began with the twelfth-century revival of agriculture, trade and town life, and has continued ever since at an accelerating rate. This explosive force has created a new type of social experience fundamental in medieval and modern times, and quite unlike the experience of the Greeks and of the Hellenistic world: the experience of an expanding society, outgrowing its older forms and institutions, and forever trying to escape their limitations. Greek philosophy, in Plato, began in an atmosphere of defeat. It sought primarily consolation. It sought it first in knowledge. Aristotle almost escaped this temper, and hence he naturally appealed most strongly to the Westerners when they began to build their first independent philosophy. Then, in the imposing religious philosophies that culminated in the Augustinian synthesis of all the currents of thought of the Mediterranean world, Hellenistic philosophizing sought consolation frankly in salvation and deliverance from the world. Modern thinking, in contrast, has never sought consolation and salvation, save for brief interludes—perhaps we are in one today. Rather, it has been the instrument of intellectual revolt, of the reconstruction of tradition, of the assimilation of new experience and thought, and of adjustment to it. Intellectually, all the problems of the medieval and modern reflection upon the religious life have arisen from the conflict of new knowledge and experience with traditional attitudes and thought. The first major clash came with the impact of Aristotelian natural science on the Augustinian, Christian Neoplatonic system of ideas in the twelfth century, an impact which at once generated all the characteristic issues involved in the "conflict between science and theology."

The moral problems of the Christian tradition in medieval and modern times have been, first, to harmonize Christian ethics with Greek humanism; and then later, to adjust the fairly successful fusion of both which Thomas Aquinas effected in the thirteenth century to the new forces of natural science and an industrial and technological world—peculiarly our own problems of moral reconstruction.

Western Europe started, in the twelfth century, in its professed ideals (though never in actual fact) with a dualistic way of life—with life as something to be escaped from. This view was embodied in Augustinian Christianity, which was a natural expression of the values of the dying Hellenistic world. This moral pattern was imposed from above on the barbarian peoples of Western Europe, as an integral part of the only civilization they knew and could find. But it was the expression of a kind of social experience totally alien to the Western Europeans. These barbarians were not dying; they possessed an immense exuberance and vitality. They were thirsting for power and prosperity, they were in love with the world and the flesh, and they were willing to go to the Devil to get them—as they have. It was natural for such a culture to be attracted to Greek thought, and to the Roman philosophy of power. It was also natural that it should be impossible for them to understand Greek thought as the Greeks did, as an aesthetic vision. They had to turn it into an instrument of power: Plato into a moral Romanticism, and Aristotle into an amoral technology.

But that Western Europeans should have tried to be Christians—that passes all human comprehension. It is as incredible as that modern Americans should ever be able to convince themselves they really ought to follow the teachings of Jesus. It is small wonder Western civilization has always found its real ideals at variance with its professed Christian dualism. Its moral history is one long record of revolt by men devoted to pleasure, prosperity, and power against even lip service to Christian ethics. The dualistic way of life has been swamped by successive waves of naturalistic ethics: the Aristotelian naturalism of Thomas Aquinas, the humanism of the Renaissance, the this-worldly asceticism of the Puritans, the rational naturalism of the eighteenth century, the irrational naturalism of the Romantic movement, the industrial and scientific naturalism of today. We have only to consider the revolt of a naturalistic ethic of power politics in men like Reinhold Niebuhr against "Christian perfectionism." And then we wonder why "Christianity has never been tried!"

The intellectual problems of Western culture have been a

similar record of successive adjustments, of traditional beliefs to new "knowledge" and "science." The first encounter was between Augustinian Neoplatonic Christian theology and Aristotelian natural science, between what the Middle Ages knew as "faith" and "reason." This began the characteristic dualism that has ever since bedeviled Western thought and Western religious ideas: between a "transcendental" but familiar world of moral and religious ideas, and an accessible but strange and frightening realm of "science." This issue was solved for the thirteenth century by Thomas Aquinas and Duns Scotus; that is why they are the first "modern" philosophers. Western philosophers have been adjusters ever since.

The problem grew still more acute when the medieval synthesis of Platonism and Aristotelianism was confronted in the seventeenth century by Alexandrian mathematical physics. The task then became to adjust the whole tradition of Greek thought to modern "natural science." This was tried first in the great seventeenth-century philosophical systems, tours de force which eighteenth-century criticism proved to have been ultimate failures. The problem was solved for Newtonian science by Kant. But in the nineteenth century the Newtonian conception of nature was abandoned by all evolutionary scientists, while the "Christian world" was abandoned by all thoughtful Christians. With both terms altered beyond recognition, the one to an evolutionary and experimental science, the other to a Christianity that no longer claims any special insight into the structure of the world, a working solution has been achieved for us in our own experimental naturalisms.

This long record of conflict and ultimate reconciliation should comfort those still bothered by its most recent form. What has been accomplished so often in the past the wit of man can still manage to effect once more. In fact, the intellectual adjustment, the conflict between scientific and religious "beliefs," would never have been taken so seriously if it had not been so deeply involved in the much more fundamental problem of adjusting conflicting values. That is still the very warp and woof of our religious perplexities today.

Both Islam and Judaism, which in the Middle Ages successively anticipated the Christians in facing these problems, found the solutions much easier. For neither was committed to identifying its religion with a set of intellectual beliefs. For both, religion was rather Law than knowledge; and though literalists and fanatics periodically protested, a Moslem or a Jewish philosopher who observed the Law could make a strong case for freedom in his intellectual beliefs. The Platonist could always reinterpret the traditional symbols in terms of Platonic thought, like Philo the Jew or Avicenna the Arab; the Aristotelian could always maintain that the ideas involved in his religious tradition were not intended to furnish truth, like Averroes the Moslem, and Maimonides the Jew. Spinoza, who in the seventeenth century so often cut through to the very essence of the medieval position of his forbears, could speak for Islam as well as for the Jewish tradition. "Between faith or theology and philosophy there is no connection or affinity. . . . Philosophy has no end in view save truth: faith, no end save obedience and piety. . . . We may take it for indisputable that theology is not bound to serve reason, nor reason theology, but that each has her own domain: reason the realm of truth and wisdom, theology that of piety and obedience. . . . Scripture does not teach philosophy, but merely obedience [to the Law], and all it contains has been adapted to the understanding and established opinions of the multitude." [1]

The Western Christians, however, were the heirs to a subtle and elaborate philosophical theology, in the thought of Augustine. Since, aside from a modicum of ancient learning transmitted in late Roman textbooks, this was the only body of systematic knowledge they knew, and by far the most impressive of all their intellectual possessions, their intellectual curiosity, awakening in the eleventh century, was naturally directed toward

[1] Spinoza, *Tractatus Theologico-Politicus,* chapters 14 and 15.

the exploration and interpretation of its imposing architecture. The title of Anselm's major theological work, *Cur Deus Homo* ("Why God Became Man"), well illustrates their initial attitude. The Incarnation they unquestioningly accepted; but how was it to be understood? The intellectual substance the Westerners found in Augustine was, of course, Christian Platonism; and their first philosophy was hence the Platonic synthesis, which they naturally identified with Christian faith. Anselm, and his successor in the twelfth century, Richard of Saint Victor, demonstrated more of the "truths" of the Christian system than any later philosophical theologian has ever dared tackle. The subsequent history of medieval rational theology was the gradual circumscribing of the field of "truths of faith" that could be proved by reason, until by the middle of the fourteenth century they had reached the vanishing point with some of the followers of William of Ockham.

Thus Western Christianity began with a complete identification of faith and reason; with the assumption that every one of its ideas could be made the subject matter of rational knowledge. God himself was identical with Truth: in Anselm's famous ontological proof, he became "that than which nothing greater can be conceived," the most inclusive of all logical universals.

But during the twelfth century Western Europe discovered Aristotelian natural science, in Moorish Spain, in Arab Sicily, and in Byzantium itself. This new body of ideas had a greater and more revolutionary impact on Christian thought than any of the subsequent new schemes of understanding that have since appeared to buffet and perplex it. The early Middle Ages possessed only dialectical skill; they had no knowledge of nature, no independent body of natural science. Their only inherited system of beliefs consisted of theological doctrines about the soul and God. Naturally they applied their dialectic to rationalize and formalize, as we should say, this Augustinian theology. The result was the Christian rationalism and Platonism of Anselm and the schools of the twelfth century, of which Chartres and Saint

Victor near Paris were outstanding. These thinkers built up a single body of Christian *Sapientia* or Wisdom. Augustine was "The Philosopher"; his system formed the body of "faith." The aim of Christian thought was to understand it, to explicate the content of "faith"—to rationalize Augustine's theology in terms of his Platonism. This enterprise was reinforced by certain other Platonic works that had come down in the Latin tradition, Dionysius the Areopagite (actually a Greek writer of the sixth century) and John Scotus Eriugena; and by the great Arabic encyclopedist and Platonic commentator on Aristotle, Avicenna. The whole adventure was intellectually dangerous, and always verging on heresy: by the beginning of the thirteenth century Amalric of Béné and David of Dinant had crossed the line into pantheistic error, and were condemned in 1215.

This Christian *Sapientia* was Platonistic in neglecting knowledge of nature; in concerning itself with the soul, the realm of Ideas, or Truth, and God; and in its method, which was intellectual vision elaborated by dialectic. Truth was to be known directly, by the Augustinian Divine Illumination of the rational soul or intellect. It was not derived from or relevant to a knowledge of empirical facts. Nature was taken as a mere set of symbols for higher truths, a book of revelation to be read for its spiritual meaning; it was interpreted, especially by the Victorines, as symbol, not analyzed as fact. Neither Anselm nor the one more questioning mind, Peter Abailard, had any use for any independent science of nature—because neither knew of any.

Into this intellectual situation Aristotelian science came as a revolutionary factor. Here was a body of independent knowledge of nature: the world was placed between the soul and God as a legitimate and valid object of knowledge. Philosophy now had a separate subject matter of its own, distinct from theology. Aristotle filled the intellectual void, and satisfied the growing curiosity about the world of nature, and the growing demand, generated by the rise of urban culture, for the expression of more humanistic values. Man was here presented, not as an

Augustinian soul condemned to the prison house of the body, but as a rational animal. This conception and all the humanistic consequences that flowed from it answered to the social experience of the new townsmen. Since Aristotle's was the only science of nature yet known, it was naturally taken as the Truth, Aristotle as "The Philosopher."

The reaction of Christian thinkers to the coming of Aristotle repeated the same reactions that had already occurred among the Moslems and the Jews. Indeed, it illustrates the typical process by which a novel body of scientific beliefs is assimilated into an older intellectual tradition: it is the pattern exemplified again and again in the subsequent history of Christian thought. First, Aristotle captivates the radicals, the innovators, and his thought begins to infiltrate the older ideas. Secondly, these changes raise opposition: the new ideas are too scientific, too empirical; Aristotle lacks all religious interest. Thirdly, Aristotle becomes the symbol of free inquiry: he is defended by determined radicals who swallow him whole, take his thought as the only truth, and forget the religious past. Fourthly, there appear mediators, modernists or compromisers, who with the help of Platonism assimilate the novel Aristotelian science to the traditional pattern of thought and values. Finally, this reconciliation and harmony of the modernists proves ultimately successful: it becomes itself the received tradition, and furnishes the starting point for the next process of assimilation. This pattern has become the familiar and oft repeated structure of the "conflict between religious faith and science."

In thirteenth-century Christendom, the radicals were the Latin Averroists who took their Aristotle straight. Averroes was the great Arabian commentator in Cordova who had held Aristotle to be the truth in philosophy and science. These radical Aristotelians, with their stronghold in the Faculty of Arts at the University of Paris and elsewhere, followed him in taking Aristotle as the final intellectual authority. In philosophy and reason, they held, there is no providence, no creation, no first man or fall of man, no personal immortality, no heaven or hell, no grace, and no sin. In other words, Aristotle was not a Christian—which seems a tenable position. In 1267 Siger de Brabant appeared at the University of Paris, to win a wide following in the Faculty of Arts. There are two conclusions, he taught, that of reason, philosophy, and Aristotle, and that of faith. The conclusions of faith are true, but those of Aristotle, reason, and philosophy are much more interesting. The aim of philosophy is to find, not the truth—that is old stuff—but what Aristotle thinks and reason can demonstrate. This was of course a denial of the rationality of the Christian tradition, a form of irrationalism or agnosticism. It proved so popular with the Masters teaching in the Faculty of Arts that Thomas Aquinas was recalled from the Papal court the same year to defend the rationality of faith.

At first, the traditionalists formed the majority, as they always do. In the face of Aristotle, and frightened by the Latin Averroists, they clung to the older medieval tradition of Augustinian Platonism. They were suspicious of the pantheism of the Arabian Aristotelians, like Avicenna; and of the scientific, empirical, nonmystical, nonreligious spirit of the Greek Aristotle. They studied Aristotle, and his commentator Averroes; they accepted much of his thought: his empirical psychology, for instance. But they insisted on the main doctrines of Augustinian Platonism. And they formed the chief opposition to the reconciling modernism of Thomas Aquinas, even in his own Dominican order.

The conciliators had two "authorities" to harmonize, Augustine and Aristotle. They hence needed to appeal to reason to learn how to do it. In consequence they initiated a vital movement: all modern religious and philosophic thought has ever since sprung from conflicts between tradition and novel ideas, and from efforts at reconciling them rationally. The problem faced by all the conciliators was the same. Here was a body of independent and certain science, obviously irrelevant to all the specifically Christian and Augustinian doctrines. How could it be kept independent, thoroughly rational and free from authority, and yet at the same time perfectly compatible with another body of knowledge quite independent of and irrelevant to it? This is the typical problem of reconciling two independent systems of ideas, one familiar and one novel, without sacrificing the values of either. It has been repeated in modern religious thought down to Kant, who offered the most impressive modern solution. This is what is called technically in philosophy "the problem of knowledge." Thomas Aquinas was more successful and sounder than Kant in his solution. Kant solved it by making science only relatively true: it does not describe "things in themselves," things as they really are. For Thomas, such a way out was impossible: he was too much of a rationalist and a scientist, too impressed by the Aristotelian conviction that the real world is intelligible. For him, science is absolutely true, and so is faith, for both alike come from God.

The solution of Thomas, foreshadowed in his teacher Albert the Great, and also foreshadowed in Avicenna and Averroes among the Moslems, and in Maimonides among the Jews, runs as follows. Reason and science are true and certain, but they are not all-comprehensive. Besides the realm of science, the "truths proposed by reason," there is a realm of faith, of "truths proposed by faith," distinct from the former, but a natural extension of it, not contrary to, but beyond "reason." Reason is certain, so far as it can go; but it is limited in its scope and power: faith furnishes more truth. Today, we are all convinced that philosophically Thomas was right: science is limited, there is always more truth to be discovered. This is the biggest contrast between Greek and modern thought; and since it begins with Albert the Great and Thomas Aquinas, they can rightly be called the first modern philosophers. But they are not at the same time modern theologians: we are not at all convinced that we have any more truth than what our limited science supplies, that we possess any superrational avenue to truth, any road other than the scientific method, broadly conceived, any absolute truth or "truths of faith."

Thomas holds that reason cannot establish or demonstrate the truths of faith. Reason can prove its own limits. But it cannot prove any of the doctrines of the Christian revelation: the Trinity, a Creation in time, the Fall, Original Sin, the Incarnation, the Sacraments, the Resurrection of the Flesh, Heaven and Hell, the Last Judgment. Because these beliefs are all true, and accepted on the basis of revelation, we know that any rational argument or science denying or conflicting with them must contain some logical fallacy. But we must demonstrate that fallacy, not by appealing to the authority of revelation, to "faith," but by reason. This remains the official Catholic position with regard, e.g., to the theory of evolution: any interpretation of the evolutionary process that denies that souls are created individually is fallacious, and must be shown to be false by rational analysis. The task of reason and science is to build up an independent true science, not contrary to the truths of faith; and to refute all false theories that are.

This is not mere conciliation and appeasement, and it is intellectually honest enough. But it is hardly free inquiry. It can be perfectly rational and consistent, but the goal is set. And where the enterprise leads near the "truths of faith," Thomas Aquinas' thought becomes a scientific and rational apologetic, at times definitely sophistical, as in dealing with the doctrine of personal immortality, for instance. For we have learned by long and sad experience with this use of knowledge as a religious apologetic, that while using methods that are perfectly "rational," by disregarding the necessary facts it is possible to "prove" what it is set out to prove. A philosophy can be completely rational and consistent, and yet give a false interpretation of experience, because of what it omits.

Thomas Aquinas furnishes the classic illustration of the second way of treating the role of knowledge and truth in the religious life, just as the Alexandrian philosophical theologians exemplify the first. There is a realm of religious truths—"truths of faith"—which are inaccessible to the methods of rational inquiry. They supplement but cannot in any sense conflict with scientific or philosophical truths, for the methods of the latter disciplines are not competent to deal with their subject-matter. To establish this important point, Thomas had to elaborate his version of the Aristotelian theory of knowledge. He turned to this Aristotelian theory because he was convinced that Platonism, both in its obviously heretical Arabian forms, and in the form of Augustine's Illumination theory of knowledge, was too dangerous to human personality and moral freedom. It was bound to lead, as it had already led so many Moslems and Christians who had embraced it, to a pantheism destructive of the dignity of human nature. That is, Thomas turned to Aristotle, not primarily to capture him for the Christian faith, but to vindicate the dignity, worth and power of human nature within that faith, and against the Augustinian supernaturalism and mysticism. What is novel and important in the philosophical theology of Thomas is not what first strikes us as we look back, as we take him for what he only became in 1879, a new scientific apologist for faith, but his drive for humanism, rationalism, and naturalism. Thomas is the great Christian humanist and Christian naturalist. He is more humanistic, and certainly far more naturalistic, than the so-called humanists of the Renaissance, whose temper wobbled between extreme optimism and utter pessimism as to human nature, and who ended with the reaffirmation of Augustine.

Thomas's Aristotelian theory of knowledge holds that man is a rational animal, and the world is a world that can be understood by reason. As rational, man can understand the universe; but as animal, he is limited to that aspect of it such an animal can experience through his senses. In his science man can know of the world only what he can learn from reflection on the facts his sense experience furnishes: he is limited by the extent of his rational observation. In what can be called Thomas's "empirical rationalism," dialectic alone can suffice to establish the existence of beings not accessible to sense experience, all "immaterial" beings. But it can do so only by showing that they form the necessary conditions of the existence of what can be so observed. "If any given thing is real," De Wulf [2] states this principle, "all other things, without which the reality of that fact would be inexplicable and unintelligible, must be no less real." The empirical element here is that we must start with a fact experienced and explain that fact; the rationalistic or dialectical element is that whatever is logically presupposed by observed facts must be true in the nature of things. There is here an implicit confidence that the pattern of human logic reproduces the structure of nature, that nature possesses a logical structure accessible to the human mind, and thus satisfies man's human scheme of intelligibility. Only philosophical idealists today, like the Neo-Orthodox, or like most religious liberals, would still make that assumption.

The consequence of this empirical rationalism for religious knowledge is that in man's knowing, the body is needed: the only human knowledge necessarily depends on materials furnished by the senses. Platonism is a sound theory of knowledge for pure intelligences, for immaterial beings like the angels and God, but not for men. The human mind perceives ideas only as embedded in sense-images. To know anything immaterial, to know God or the angels, man must start from facts delivered to sense experience; and he can go only so far as is necessary to understand those facts of observation. "God," for example, is not to be reached through the soul alone, as Augustine and the mystics held, but only by rational inference from the data of the senses. God's existence can indeed be demonstrated, but only as the necessary presupposition of a First Cause for effects observable in experience, like motion or order.

In such a framework, "God" naturally ceases to be a warm reality, a living presence, and becomes a scientific principle, a

[2] Maurice De Wulf, *Philosophy and Civilization in the Middle Ages,* p. 215.

rational conclusion. In Thomas Aquinas's natural or rational theology, the proofs of God's existence establish such principles as the laws of nature. The "Prime Mover" and "Necessary Being" are like the laws of thermodynamics or the law of the conservation of energy: they are the first principles of a scientific postulate system. Made mathematical, they become Spinoza's order of nature. They constitute a scientific rationalism as the framework for religious feeling. That is, Thomas is a typical modernist, in identifying the object of religious emotion and aspiration with the first principles of his science. He thus achieves a harmony of aspiration and knowledge—and also, in Paul Tillich's phrase, like all natural theologians, a "broken myth."

In Aristotle as in Thomas this empirical rationalism was a protest against the claim of the Platonists to a direct and internal vision of Truth. But for Aristotle it was a sober statement of fact about man and his way of securing contact with the universe, not a limitation of knowledge. For in Aristotle's world there was nothing that could not enter into man's experience. But Thomas was a Christian: he knew, by faith, that he was living in the universe of Augustine. And in that Christian universe there was much that no mere rational animal could possibly experience. Thus Thomas's empiricism set limits to human knowledge in the interest of preserving a realm where only revelation was competent to furnish truth. It created for him the problem of adjusting "faith" to "reason," of harmonizing what is revealed to Christian souls with what a rational animal can experience. For Thomas, a thoroughly humanistic and naturalistic view of man, and of man's natural knowledge and natural moral power, is set squarely in the midst of the traditional Christian, Augustinian Neoplatonic universe. He thus remained an "extra-naturalist," a "superrationalist." This is what is meant by calling Thomas a conciliator, a mediator, a modernist. This is why there must be for him the two realms of "faith" and of "reason," and why there must be both a natural or rational theology, based on his scientific principles, and a revealed theology, which furnishes special religious knowledge of God and man. Thomas succeeded in effecting a consistent and harmonious adjustment between the two, an ordered, neatly articulated hierarchy, by dividing the "truths proposed by reason" from the "truths proposed by faith."

Thomas freed science from domination by Christian theology, and made reason and philosophy, within their own realm, independently true. But his enterprise of making reason independent of authority and separate from faith, of making reason and faith exclude each other, of making philosophy and revealed theology quite separate sciences, inevitably led beyond modernism. Modernism, the attempt to harmonize new ideas with old, to put new wine in old bottles, cannot afford to become dogmatic or crystalized: there can be no final assimilation of growing knowledge. By separating and adjusting nicely the two reams of faith and science, one can always avoid any specific conflict; but the adjustment will never stay put. Faith can always be fitted to any particular body of scientific ideas; but there can be no permanent fitting to free inquiry. This the Thomists have found out, as have the Kantians. This explains the Catholic predicament: once start on this path, and you have to keep on. If you stop with the first adjustment, you are intellectually worse off than before. You soon find you are now tied not only to the "truths of faith," but also to an antiquated science as well—the Catholics, to Thomas's Aristotelian physics and cosmology, the Kantians, to Newtonian mechanics and Euclidian geometry. That is why the second way of construing the role of knowledge and truth in the religious life, through the notion of a special and privileged "religious knowledge," has never proved ultimately satisfying, and has in the end always given way to either the first or the third positions: to a consistently rational philosophical theology, or to the view that there is no theoretical "truth" at all in religion.

The development after Thomas was actually in the latter direction. Thomism was never really popular in the later Middle Ages. Too naturalistic for the conservatives, and too much of a compromising philosophical theology for the radicals, it retreated largely into the Dominican order, till the Jesuits revived it around 1550. John Duns Scotus soon became the most influential conservative religious philosopher. He held this position for some two and a half centuries, until the Council of Trent. A careful and penetrating critic, he reconstructed the Thomist positions in the light of an Augustinian Platonism. With a rigorous Platonic ideal of mathematical demonstration, he found most of the Thomistic natural theology only relatively valid: the typical Thomistic "proofs" for the existence of God from his effects in experience are not conclusive demonstrations. The field of rationally demonstrable knowledge is much more limited for Scotus than for Thomas, and philosophy is more widely separated from theology. Many of God's attributes—his omnipotence, his goodness, his providence—are indemonstrable. The special creation and the immortality of the soul are likewise incapable of rational proof: it cannot be proved that the soul can exist apart from the body, or that it needs future rewards and punishments. Vice is its own punishment, and virtue its own reward. The desire for immortality proves nothing, if it be not possible. Theology, in fact, is not a theoretical science, but only a practical science, furnishing not knowledge but, rather, norms for conduct. Nothing revealed is capable of demonstration. Scotus's own rational theology finds it necessary to posit an infinite, unlimited Being, a "first" in the order of Being, an ultimate End, and an ultimate in the order of Perfection: three "primalities" in all. The *Theoremata,* which if not by Scotus himself seems to be a Scotist work, is a penetrating critique of natural theology, fully as sceptical of its pretensions as Ockham.

William of Ockham became the radical, scientific, and nonreligious philosopher of the later Middle Ages. He is a thoroughgoing empiricist as to matters of fact: nothing is real or valid in existence that is not an observed fact or a relation between observed facts. This "razor," when applied to natural theology and rational psychology, had electrifying results. All theology belongs to "faith," not to reason and science. Revelation is true:

"believe" it. But do not weaken it by attempted pseudo demonstrations that are bound to fall short of rigorous proof. Realize that in theology there is nothing that can be theoretically proved or demonstrated. In his *Commentary on the Sentences* Ockham admits the proof of a First Efficient Cause of motion, though, since it is not clear that an infinite temporal series of past causes is impossible, it is more advisable to prove a First Sustainer of the universe in the present, where an infinite regress is clearly logically impossible. But a "Supreme Being" cannot be proved. In his *Centiloquium Theologicum* Ockham considers any argument for a Prime Mover impossible: at most it is only "probable," not demonstrative. Things do move themselves: angels, souls, even heavy bodies. An infinite series of causes is possible. Hence the Prime Mover is strictly indemonstrable. There is no proof of any attribute of God, even of his unity: logically there may be several Gods, and Gods of other universes are quite possible, so that God's unity is only probable. Likewise his infinity, which is indemonstrable and only probable. Indeed, all of God's attributes are mere names: in God there is no real distinction between his intellect and his will.

In psychology, there is no proof of the existence of a substantial and immaterial soul. Introspection reveals only mental states, and our different intellectual operations, nothing more. There is neither intuitive nor demonstrative knowledge of the Aristotelian "active intellect," much less of its supposed immortality. By reason we can demonstrate only that the soul is an extended, material, and corruptible form of the body; we cannot know by reason or by experience alone, without "faith," that we possess an immaterial soul which is the form of the human body. Moral principles are not logically necessary, but are pure commands of God: there is no such thing as a rational or natural morality. Ockham has no reservations about the first two commandments, like the Scotists. God could have commanded hatred, murder, or adultery, had he wanted to, and it would have then been our moral duty to obey his will.

With Ockham we arrive at the position that there is no rational knowledge or truth whatsoever in theology: everything is "revealed." The Aristotelian natural theology so bravely launched by Albert and Thomas has failed. It is no longer true that "faith" furnishes us a separate religious knowledge which supplements what reason can give, as Thomas held. It furnishes us no theoretical "knowledge" at all. Religious ideas and beliefs are nonrational though justified instruments of salvation. And we must remember that this position was maintained, not in the eighteenth-century French *salons,* but in the fourteenth-century Christian universities of Europe. For two hundred years such Ockhamism was the dominant philosophy in the Schools. The turning to mysticism, and to the completely irrational "faith" of the great Reformers, was clearly inevitable. Ockham's influence led to two centuries of scepticism in metaphysics, and fideism in theology. It is interesting to observe today how often history repeats itself.

Some of the later Ockhamites went on to an even more devastating philosophical scepticism. Typical is Jean Gerson, in the early fifteenth century. Brought up in this sceptical empiricism, he tried for a while to reconcile it with the religious rationalism of the Scotists. Then, convinced that this was the outcome of reason and science, he fell back on an Augustinian mysticism. The great speculative mystics of the end of the fourteenth century, Suso, Tauler, and Meister Eckhart, equally represented a reaction to the second position away from this failure of medieval rational theology and religion. And Luther, who was educated as an Ockhamite by Gabriel Biel, drank in his teacher's contempt for the "harlot, reason" from just such Ockhamite strictures on the power of reason and science to achieve any results in thinking about religious problems. He, too, drew deeply on the great fourteenth-century mystics. And like Calvin, and the other Reformers, he returned to Augustine's formulation of Christian thought for a fresh start. Aristotelian science was no longer taken seriously by religious thinkers, though it lingered on for a century in academic circles, and in Italy developed rapidly into Galilean science. The Christian beliefs were freed from the incubus of the now abandoned Aristotelian natural theology, to meet the incursion of a fresh, and, it seemed at first, an even more dangerous body of scientific ideas.

It was Galilean science, the new mathematical and mechanical interpretation of nature of the seventeenth century, usually considered the first great wave of the modern scientific enterprise, which restored men's confidence in reason once more, now in a reason made wholly mathematical. This in turn made possible another major attempt at philosophical theology and rational religion, the second in the history of Western culture. For every new scheme of understanding the world, every new body of scientific ideas, by raising the ever fresh hope that at last the secrets of the universe have been penetrated, at once leads to a reinterpretation of traditional religious symbols and beliefs in its terms, and produces a new wave of speculative theology. When faith in Newtonian science as the open sesame faded in turn, and men went on to the novel scheme of the Romantic idealistic philosophies, rational theology found one more rebirth, in the great Hegelian systems. When "evolution" became the key word, and all thought was rewritten in temporal and genetic terms, there was another spate of speculative "evolutionary" theologies. In an intellectual culture like that of the West, such attempts at philosophical theology are doubtless inevitable. They have their values, as we have seen in the first Christian instance, the Trinity. At the very worst, we must acknowledge that God must like them: he provokes men to generate so many.

Yet it used to be the fashion a generation ago to conceive the relation of science to religion entirely in terms of their purely incidental and surface "conflicts." The conservatives are right: science is indeed a perpetual peril to theology. But the real dangers to religious thinking have come actually not from any frontal attack by irreligious scientific ideas. They have come rather from insidious and conspiratorial subversion from within the theological fold itself. When scientific ideas stand in open opposition to religious beliefs, the worst they can do is to make faith seem literally false or even irrelevant, judged by narrowly "scientific" standards. But when embraced by religious thinkers themselves, half-understood scientific conceptions can issue in a blasphemous corruption of all sound theology. What science really produces in religious thought is not heresy or loss of faith, but blasphemy.

The clearest illustration of this religious maxim is the new Cartesian and Newtonian rational religion that came to dominate religious thinking in the seventeenth and eighteenth centuries. This Newtonian "scientific religion" ultimately failed, as had the earlier rational religion of the Aristotelians, and with far more of justification. That failure sent some religious men in the Romantic movement to a new scheme of understanding and hence a new rational and philosophical theology, in the Absolute Idealism of Hegel. But far more significantly, it led certain pioneer religious thinkers to try to found religion on something other than scientific truth, or indeed any kind of cognitive truth. Thus was effected, in the great Romantic philosophical reinterpretations of the nature and function of religion, the most profound of all the revolutions in the place accorded knowledge and truth in Christianity. It is a revolution which the later scientific and historical study and analysis of religion has merely spelt out in detail.

But while it lasted, the "scientific religion" of the Cartesians and the Newtonians almost wrecked the Christian tradition, by identifying it completely with a form of rational knowledge. During the Age of Reason Western culture learned many things of momentous significance. And one of the most conclusive of all its lessons was how *not* to reconcile science and religion. The two cannot be brought together in harmony by trying to found religion on scientific beliefs. That way spells disaster for both great human enterprises. This lesson was well worth its cost. And the cost was great: men wasted much time and thought

during the Romantic era in the not unnatural alternative of trying to found science on religion.

The new scientists, from Copernicus to Newton, were hardly
irreligious men. They were quite sincere in the belief that in
finding "the plan by which the universe was made" they were
adding new glory to the Maker. With this conviction themselves,
it was all the easier for them to make the natural attempt to
render their new ideas of nature palatable, by emphasizing the
strong support the rational apologetic of the new science would
bring to religious faith. Some of them, like Copernicus and
Kepler, were philosophically Platonists, who felt they were read-
ing the mathematical structure by which nature shadowed forth
and participated in the Divine Logos. Others, like Galileo and
most of the Italians, were philosophically Aristotelians, who held
to the Thomistic view of the relation of science to faith (stated
in Galileo's letter to the Grand Duchess Christine): that since
both come from God their respective truths cannot be at variance.
Both groups employed the common figure, that men had at last
succeeded in discovering the language in which the Book of
Nature is written, which is mathematical.

The philosophers who generalized and extended the new
science and tried to assimilate it to the intellectual tradition, were
led, not against their own wills, into a new speculative theology.
Descartes, who drew upon a variety of traditional theological
ideas as the support and bulwark of his new mechanistic philosophy of nature, including a theory of knowledge based on
Augustinian Platonism, and Scotist voluntarism, together with
the Molinist doctrine of the freedom of the will of the Jesuits,
built God into the very foundation of that philosophy, as the
continual Sustainer of the universe. In his enormously influential
Discourse on Method he made God the ultimate epistemological
guarantee, and initiated that pernicious strain in modern philosophical theology which finds epistemology the royal road to
the Divine. Descartes was, in fact, a pious physicist—than which,

as we have learned again of late, there can be no greater sub-
verter of all sound theology. He was always convinced that God
had sent his Angel of Truth to him personally in the famous
vision in the upper chamber, as a personal guarantee of his
rightness. This was the source of what Henry More aptly called
his "inexsuperable confidence" in his own ideas. Descartes had
a characteristically Augustinian experience of direct illumination
by the Logos, without any institutional intermediary. This helped
make Cartesianism so potent a force in breaking the intellectual
authority of the Church. He vowed and completed a pilgrimage
to Loretto in gratitude to the God of Truth.

Leibniz, the pure mathematician in all things, treated theology
as a postulate system whose assumptions he could freely manipu-
late. In the interests of harmonizing and reconciling all parties
and all ideas, he worked out a new speculative mathematical
theology that proved enormously influential in the eighteenth
century, and indeed furnished the main outlines, minus Leibniz's
own original and suggestive mathematical ideas, of the rational
theology of many of the great Romantic thinkers.

The two most penetrating religious philosophers of the
seventeenth century were Spinoza and Hobbes. Spinoza used
the new scientific scheme of understanding to construct a rational
philosophical theology that would give the true interpretation of
traditional religious symbols and beliefs. He illustrates as fully
as the Alexandrian Doctors the identification of religion with
true knowledge—the first of our three positions. For Spinoza, as
for Bacon, knowledge is power; but for him it is the power to
bring salvation and human freedom. He was completely convinced that Cartesian science had at last provided the answers for
all the traditional medieval theological problems. It had taught
him what God really is, and man, and human welfare and blessed-
ness. Traditional beliefs, in the Scriptures and elsewhere, gave
no knowledge, but only fostered piety and obedience to the Law.
His reward for answering the medieval intellectual problems of
religion with complete and thoroughgoing honesty and truth was

to be dubbed an atheist. For he preserved the very substance of medieval religion, its piety and its scheme of otherworldly values, in an age in which men were already in full revolt against that substance. He did not care to maintain its superficial forms, which men still wished to observe.

As Spinoza represents the very essence of medieval piety, interpreted in a framework of the latest scientific ideas—the Cartesian scheme which he judged to be the final truth about nature—so Hobbes represents the essence of Reformation and Puritan self-abnegation, thoroughly naturalized in the Galilean world of bodies in motion. He shares the Calvinistic view of the natural man, and of God as pure power and will, wholly opaque to reason. He shares its denial of all natural and rational theology, and its conviction that salvation must come to man from outside, from complete surrender to a Power far greater than any man— to that great Leviathan, the State: "There is no power on earth that can compare with it." For him, too, theology is not knowl- edge, but Law, a means of governing men; and the attributes of God are "names"—the nominalistic term for "symbols"—a means of honoring God, not knowing him. Hobbes thus ex- emplifies completely the third of our three positions. He quarreled with the Puritans over the proper Church polity (he was a con- firmed Erastian) but not over the essence of their common faith. He bent their vision of God and man to the service of what was to become the strongest religion of modern times, the religion of the State.

As there were two waves of the new science, so there were two major types of rational theology, Cartesian and Newtonian. The seventeenth century, having discovered the mathematical and rational Order of Nature, identified that order with God. Of this first type, the best expressions are Spinoza and the Male- branche who shared the same vision and the same rational theology, though he employed the Christian and Augustinian terminology and symbols. But with Newton, God had ceased to be the Order of Nature, and had become its First Cause and

Original Force. God was no longer, as for Spinoza, the ultimate Formal Cause of the Universe, but now figured as its First Efficient Cause, and in a temporal, non-Aristotelian sense. Newton, another pious physicist, who spent much time in Biblical commentary, especially on the apocalyptic books, proclaimed some individual blasphemies which he had learned from Henry More, the Cambridge Platonist. God by existing constituted Absolute Space and Absolute Time, which together formed the Divine Sensorium, or sense organ. His will was the ether that kept the heavenly bodies from getting into a huddle in the center of his mind—Space—through universal gravitation, and that corrected the mathematical irregularities in the celestial movements he had not been able to elucidate. But the tremendous influence of Newton on the rational theology of the Age of Reason was his identification of the Deity with the original Creator of the great perpetual motion machine. God was the great Designing Force; and since such an ultimate concept was demanded by Newton's philosophy of nature, if scarcely by his "natural philosophy" or science—"it must be the effect of counsel," Newton put it—God seemed firmly rooted in "the plan by which the universe was made." It was not till God designed events like the Lisbon earthquake that earnest Deists like Voltaire began to have their doubts.

Two complete and utter failures of Enlightenment thinking led directly to the overthrow of the universal sway of the Newtonian scientific ideal: the catastrophes that eventuated when men tried to reduce religion and art to forms of rational thought. The rise and fall of the popular rational or scientific religion of the Age of Reason represents the second great attempt to adapt the religious tradition of the West to the forces of modern life. The first attempt, undertaken in the Renaissance and the Reformation, had concentrated on the assimilation of the new values of modern social experience: it welcomed individualism, commercialism, this-worldliness. This absorption of novel values proved and has remained highly successful. But intellectually the Renaissance was too radical: it provoked a medieval reaction against the modernizing Papacy. It left the Puritans, both Catholic and Protestant, in their intellectual beliefs in the world of Augustine, minus its Platonic philosophy, which both Calvin and the Jesuits rejected. But in their values they were now living with commerce, profit-seeking, business enterprise, and the rigid discipline of free competition.

The second attempt at coming to terms with modern culture made central the intellectual assimilation of Newtonian science, though the shifting social values of the Enlightenment were also incorporated, especially the lessening of the Puritan this-worldly asceticism, in response to increasing material prosperity. So long as the Newtonian world kept the allegiance of thoughtful men, this intellectual adjustment effected in "natural religion" was highly successful: rational religion was universally popular between 1700 and 1750. To be sure, religion lost all values but that of furnishing ultimate scientific categories; but at least it was "scientific" and "rational." Then "rational theology" suddenly collapsed completely in the face of the devastating critique of those concepts advanced by empiricists like Hume, Holbach, and Kant. The very success of Protestantism in becoming in the Age of Reason completely individualistic and rationalistic turned into its greatest liability during the ensuing age of nationalistic and industrial collectivism.

From Lord Herbert of Cherbury in 1624 to William Paley in 1798, "rational religion" turned to science as the way out from the theological controversies of the Puritan age. Locke's primary motive in his influential *The Reasonableness of Christianity* (1695) was to escape from quarreling theologians, so that men might get down to business. Rational religion posed two new tests for the tradition: its practical utility and its scientific reasonableness. Of what earthly use is religion? Will it make a man any the better citizen? What in religion aids a rational, socially useful life?

If a man once admits the existence of a God, the reality of moral good and evil, the immortality of the soul, future rewards and punishments, what need has he of prejudices? Supposing him initiated in all the mysteries of transubstantiation, consubstantiation, the Trinity, hypostatical union, predestination, incarnation, and the rest, will he be any the better citizen? [3]

Secondly, what in religion gives a scientifically true explanation of things?

Judged by these two tests, religion became a set of "scientific" propositions offering an incentive to the social virtues of an individualistic society. Out of all the wealth of aspiration, feeling, emotion, expression, symbolism and poetry of the great Christian tradition, men looked to it for the two things it had never pretended to give: scientific truth and the pattern of business success. This is really extraordinary. We have hardly yet gotten over its disastrous effects. We still think the Jewish-Christian tradition must somehow furnish an adequate intellectual explanation of the world. And when we discover it does not, we are tempted to judge, it must then be of no value. Or we still imagine that Christian-Jewish ethics will solve all our moral problems in an industrial and technological world. And we hardly dare contemplate the possibility that it may not suffice.

What could pass these two tests became the "religion of reason"; what in the tradition was left over was "revelation." Three tenets were accepted as the essence of rational theology by the overwhelming body of educated men: the existence of God, his command of a moral law, and rewards and punishments in a future life. Two major controversies ensued. The supernatural rationalists, who accepted both rational theology and revelation, first argued with the Deists, who held to "rational theology" alone, over whether revelation was necessary in addition to natural theology. The Deists then argued with the "sceptics" (who embraced both fideists and atheists) over whether rational theology could itself be demonstrated.

On the first issue, the necessity of revelation, the Deists in-

[3] Diderot, *Oeuvres*, ed. Assézat et Tourneux, I, 182; quoted in John Morley, *Diderot and the Encyclopedists* (London, 1914), I, 72.

sisted that a universal God would not give a single, exclusive revelation. "How odd of God to choose the Jews!" The argument here is in Matthew Tindal, *Christianity as Old as Creation* (1730). Secondly, the content of revelation is irrational, and of no earthly use in fostering virtue. Thirdly, the positive, "external" evidence for revelation breaks down. Anthony Collins criticised the argument from "prophesies"; William Woolston and David Hume, that from "miracles." Hume's *Essay on Miracles* contrasts the weakness of a single reported experience of a supposed miracle with the force of a universal experience of natural law: a miracle can be accepted only when "the fallibility of the witness would be a greater miracle." The uniformity of nature, that basic tenet of the Newtonian faith, was the chief obstacle. The faith in miracles was destroyed not by a sceptical "empiricism," but by the rational faith in the order of nature; it had been denied by rationalists like Spinoza and Malebranche a century before. It was impossible to believe in both science and miracles.

The validity of natural theology itself posed a more searching issue. The arguments for the existence of God as a Newtonian ultimate principle, as a scientific explanation, were destroyed by Hume in the name of empiricist methods; and by Holbach and Kant, by empiricist reasoning. Those arguments had developed in the setting of the Newtonian philosophy of nature, and as scientific concepts they were valid only within that setting. "There must be a First Efficient Cause" depends on generalizing the position of philosophical mechanism, together with the assumption that the only "cause" of motion must be force. "There must have been an intelligent Creator" depends on the necessity of a "cause" of order, "design." The argument for a moral order follows the analogy of the physical order—and the outcome here was, "Whatever is, is right." Hume showed that only a "cause" for the world as a whole that is as little intelligent and good as the observed facts justify can be validly inferred. No new facts can be derived from this "teleological" argument—that God is all good, for example. The real question is, "Is there any distributive justice observable here below?" The argument from the analogy of the world to an unfinished work is very weak; for we have no other experience of the supposed Creator than just these "unfinished" works. The argument to a First Cause can at best establish only a finite, imperfect, plural Deity. And the problem of evil either robs God of all character, as in Calvin, or is rationally insoluble. Hume concluded, "Our most holy religion is founded not on knowledge but on faith." The outcome was either atheism, as with the anticlerical French, like Holbach; or sheer fideism, as with most of the British—a position shared by Joseph Butler's *Analogy of Religion,* and approached even by Kant.

It is clear that the failure of the Enlightenment attempt to harmonize religion and science was due to its trying to reduce religion to a kind of science itself. The result was that the whole world of religious values was lightly thrown overboard. And the Romanticism that rejected this entire enterprise was really a reaction, not against Hume and Holbach—Kant could admit their criticisms of rational theology gladly—but against Newton, and Locke, and a "Reasonable Christianity" as "Old as Creation" and "Not Mysterious." It was a reaction against the disintegrating effects of pseudoscientific liberalism and modernism in religion, of trying to reduce religion to what could be validly established as "knowledge," not against atheism or scepticism. The rational religion of the Enlightenment seems a perfect example of how *not* to reconcile religion and science. It has the great advantage of offering a complete episode. And every liberal religious thinker, facing the same problem of reconciliation today, would do well to study it most carefully. Whatever their shortcomings, the liberal Neo-Orthodox have learned this lesson.

The Romantic reaction led not only to the great revivals of traditional religion in the early part of the nineteenth century— British evangelicalism, the strengthening of German pietism, the rebirth of the Catholic faith. Even in the sophisticated schemes of understanding of philosophic idealism, which were anything but traditional, what was set forth in novel terms was still a religious view of the universe. There was something, not inappropriately symbolized as "God," supporting man and his values: "a Friend behind phenomena." There was a cosmic process of Providence by which God's growing creation was guided onward and upward. Hence the wide revival of the scientific faith and ideal in the middle of the century came with an especial shock to those who had grown up in the warm embrace of this cosmic religious optimism, a shock that would hardly have been felt by the earlier Calvinists.

That revival came in large part from the steady working out and carrying further of the concepts of mechanistic science which had been in the world since the seventeenth century. They had gained in power, sweep, and effectiveness with the transformation of the older Newtonian approach into the now all-conquering "hypothetico-experimental" method, which itself owed so much to the very Romantic critique of the narrowness and limitations of the Newtonian scheme and concepts. The great theoretical generalizations of the first part of the century were too impressive to ignore. When they were joined by the developmental and genetic hypotheses which seemed to give a scientific answer to the one question Newton had left for God, "How did it all start and come about?" religious men realized they must somehow come to terms with this new expanding cosmos of scientific theory.

The new "conflicts" with science struck home especially to those who had trusted Newton, identified God's function with creation, and still preserved an innocent confidence in the creation myths of Genesis. First in the nebular hypothesis of the origin of the solar system; then in the spread of uniformitarian ideas in geology, with the revolutionary changes in notions of the formation and the age of the earth they brought; and finally in the theory of the biological origin of species, it became clear that science was presenting a powerful alternative to the apologetic notion of "intelligent design." The literal-minded were shocked, as they had been in the twelfth century when they discovered through Greek science that despite Joshua the world is round. They felt at first that all force had been stolen from the "teleological argument" for God's existence. But it took only a little thought to realize that this grand genetic and evolutionary process was itself the very essence of natural teleology. It was in fact the first great reinstatement of functional and teleological concepts into the body of scientific ideas since their expulsion by Descartes. Actually, in the very heart of the mechanistic world, teleology had been installed once more. Here was Providence reclothed as the latest scientific idea! And if Providence come, can God be far behind? The one traditional religious concept that found no support in the new science was the idea of personal survival. Hence for the first time personal immortality became the chief bone of contention between the religious tradition and the new scientific faith, a place it still holds for some belated sleepers.

The biological origin of human nature and of man, associated with the name of Darwin, was of all these intellectual changes destined to have the most momentous effects, when its consequences were fully worked out. It proved most shocking to the Christian Platonists, especially to the adherents of the imposing German philosophical idealisms, sophisticated reconstructions of the earlier tradition of Augustinian Platonism. It would hardly have shocked the Hebrews, for whom man was also made of the dust of the earth. And to the Aristotelians it should have seemed old stuff to learn that man had become a rational animal once more. But the real meaning of taking man as a natural product, as a living being endowed with intelligence dwelling in an environment that has created and fostered him, which is what "rational animal" means, remained to be worked out in the next century, in our contemporary philosophical experimental naturalisms. It was obscured for a full generation by a great new upsurge of the impulse to speculative theology. This was the era of the impressive evolutionary religions, which perceived fully the value of the newly discovered process of cosmic and human development for a new venture at rational theology. Evolution was God's way of doing things, proclaimed John Fiske. Henry Drummond, in contrast to Darwin, depicted *The Ascent of Man.* More technical philosophers, impatient of the now antiquated terminology of philosophical idealism, worked out imposing theories of "creative evolution." The great appeal, in fact, of the idea of cosmic evolution was not as a sober scientific theory, but as a new Romantic faith about the universe as a whole and about man as the culmination of its long development. And how the new evolutionary theologians murdered the concept of a precise "evolution" as an exact scientific instrument to make it appeal!

The most familiar English and American theologians of creative evolution are Lloyd-Morgan, Samuel Alexander, Whitehead, and Dewey. Their thought and their enterprise are in undeserved disrepute today. This is not for intellectual or philosophic reasons. Creative evolution is still the best scientific interpretation of the Christian symbols taken as a cosmic faith, as a speculative theology. They are in disrepute because the values of nineteenth-century hope in the future they enshrined have seemed to turn sour in our own Age of Anxiety. "They did not know enough about human nature"—so the judgment of our present-day "philosophical anthropologists" in their wisdom runs. Only the Marxians, whose own "historical materialism" is one version of creative evolution, and who notoriously make plenty of use of the Christian ideas, if not of Christian symbols, still believe in an automatic progress in the good old-fashioned Victorian sense. But the bourgeois creative evolutionists, believe it or not, had heard of sin and evil, before Reinhold Niebuhr was born. While the history of the last generation has scarcely furnished additional grounds for uncritical optimism, it has hardly destroyed man's hope of making progress through his own strenuous efforts.

Indeed, the grounds for pessimism today no longer lie in anything our science claims to know about the cosmos. They have been laid squarely at man's own door, and are due solely to difficulties of his own making. Man's innate cussedness has in

Whitehead's phrase rather greater perceptive insistence today than it demanded before 1914. But far greater also is our understanding of human nature and the forces and influences that produce that cussedness. We can scarcely as yet claim to have discovered the cure; but neither can Paul or Augustine, Luther or Calvin. In a cartoon published in Germany shortly after 1918, God appears in a cloud to remark to Wilson, "They don't seem to be paying much attention to your Fourteen Points." The President of the United States, who was not lacking in all brightness, even in German eyes, came back: "Neither have they ever paid much attention to your Ten." It is only to religious emotion and conviction of sin, not to speak of obvious homiletic demands, that the cussedness of human nature seems wholly incurable. If we can manage to keep from blowing ourselves into atomic dust, which is perhaps still doubtful, we can look forward to making some headway with what is after all an intellectual, and technological, or therapeutic, problem.

The nineteenth-century scientific ideas which seemed to threaten a cosmic pessimism (like the second law of thermodynamics, which so pleased cynics like the Adams family) have ceased to trouble us. The universe, we are now reassured, will give us Great Apes time to show whether we can really make good, if we can only keep from committing suicide. Those cosmic generalizations are now seen to be not iron laws of nature, but methodological assumptions. And the whole of natural science now appears to us, in our present-day critical philosophies of science and scientific method, not as a direct rendering of the structure of the universe, as the seventeenth-century pioneers felt in their initial enthusiasm, and not as the only possible way the human mind possesses of understanding its experience, as Kant, bound to the limitations of a single and unchanging Newtonian scheme, was convinced. It is a body of assumptions and postlates, of hypotheses and theories, which is developing and changing today more rapidly than ever before, and which enables us mortals to organize our ascertained knowledge of certain highly selected aspects of the experienced world, and to formulate questions that will direct further inquiry, and thus lead to the revision of those assumptions and postulates.

Natural science, in a word, is a scheme of understanding the world which man, in cooperation with the world's structure and forces, has managed to work out with some startling success—in the particular fields it has selected to understand. Those fields do not include man's more complex cultural and spiritual experience. There we must learn all we can from the successful methods of the natural sciences. But a real understanding of the moral life, of human society, of art and poetry, and of religion, is an undertaking which in each case must stand on its own feet. This enterprise of exploring and analyzing the great cultural institutions of mankind leads us to see more clearly their role in the human and social experience of man. And here it is not the natural sciences, with their very inappropriate techniques and procedures, but the attempts to find more adequate schemes of intelligibility that will really enable us to deal with such complex experience, which are the most pertinent and suggestive. It now seems to us laughable, were it not so tragic, that natural science could ever have seemed to come into conflict with any of the other great human enterprises, like religion, with which it forms a fellowship.

Our understanding of human nature and our understanding of religion itself may well conflict with our accustomed ideas about how to think in the religious life. At the moment they do present important intellectual issues. But it is clear that while thoughtful religious men will understand the world in terms of our best scientific conclusions about it, it is not truth about the world, natural science, that furnishes the knowledge that must play a vital role in the practice by intelligent men of the religious life. It is to the relation between religion and the fruitful analyses of human experience effected during the last century and a half, first in the great Romantic interpretations of the nature and function of religion, and then in our accumulating if hardly definitive science of man's cultural life, that we must now turn.

Chapter Three. *Religion and Human Experience*

Religion, men learned by bitter experience in the Age of Reason, was not to be reduced to knowledge, to a set of rational propositions demonstrated by the accredited method of science. "Rational religion," the attempt at a scientific religion worked out on the model, and by means of the method, of Newtonian "reason," proved in the eighteenth century a complete and utter failure. Not only, as Hume conclusively showed, was the "demonstration," judged by its own scientific standards, a fraud; in the process of reducing religion to the pseudo science of "natural theology," the essence of the religious life, all spiritual values, inevitably evaporated. To be sure, the enthusiastic application of the same narrow and inadequate scientific method to the other great enterprises of human life, the construing of moral experience and the practice of art and poetry in terms of the assumptions of Newtonian mechanics, led to an equal failure. The moral life likewise eluded the confines of scientific demonstration, and artistic creation could not be bound by rational rules.

This debacle led to a reaction against the overenthusiastic misapplication of the scientific ideal. If that "reason" proved a broken reed in these great areas of human activity, to what could men turn for further light and for an instrument of criticism? The failure of the scientific ideal of reducing all men's enterprises to rational knowledge led to the Romantic reaction.[1] That is,

[1] The vexed term "Romantic" is here used in the most general sense, to designate an entire intellectual period or era, and to embrace the whole movement of reaction against the Newtonian ideal of reason, and the fresh appeal to human experience it ushered in. Thus Kant is taken as a part of that intellectual movement, since his "critical philosophy" provided the justification for its reinterpretations of experience. Actually, of course, Kant's thought may be equally regarded as the culmination of eighteenth-

men turned, as they had turned so often before in criticism of a too narrow "reason," back to human experience. Newtonian "reason" with its mechanistic assumptions, powerful as it seemed in penetrating the secrets of nature, could not be the whole story about the life of man. Indeed, it had proved incapable of making intelligible even the human enterprise of Newtonian mechanics itself. As Hume showed, not only our most holy religion but even our most useful science turned out to be founded on faith. Such fideism might satisfy the Royal Society, as Whitehead has pointed out. But it did not satisfy poets and artists, moral prophets, reflective theologians or philosophers trying to understand the cultural life of man. They might be dissatisfied with the "reason" of Newtonian science, but they were not prepared to abandon all attempts to understand, or to reject all intellectual illumination and all critical standards. Religion was indeed not identical with knowledge, but for them knowledge still had an essential role to play in the religious life. What was clearly needed was a new conception of "reason," a new intellectual method.

Kant was here the great liberator. Like Thomas Aquinas confronted with Aristotelian science, he parceled out fields for different methods. He drew the boundaries between, on the one hand, what Thomas called "natural reason," and what he himself called

---

century rationalism; and his critical philosophy is to be clearly distinguished from "philosophic idealism," and certainly from what is often called "Romantic idealism."

This comprehensive use of "Romantic" is in general accord with American usage, which not only includes Kant and Hegel, but takes Nietzsche and the later Existentialism as the expression of the same philosophic impulse. The Germans, of course, use "Romantic" in a much more restricted sense, excluding both Kant and Hegel, and focusing upon what they call *die Romantik,* of which tendency Novalis would be the great exemplar.

This broad connotation becomes important in this chapter. For Albrecht Ritschl is taken as the illustration of the third major "Romantic" reinterpretation of religion. Philosophically he was a Kantian, and he lived during the middle portion of the last century. But the construing of religion he elaborated had taken form during the earlier generation, in Fichte and indeed in Kant himself. Ritschl was the most influential spokesman of this position in theological circles. Those who object to placing him in the general "Romantic" movement are quite free to adopt another terminology.

the "understanding" based on "scientific experience"; and, on the other, the "pure" or "transcendental" reason that could deal with ethics, religion, and art. By showing the limits of the Newtonian scheme of understanding, he set forth how human experience could find intelligible place, as it obviously finds practical ones, for the creative activities of the artist and poet, for the life of moral obligation, and, though he was as relentless as Hume on the pretensions of any "natural theology," for an ethical religion founded on man's moral experience. The limitations of Kant's own analysis, which are obvious enough today, all spring from his identification, natural for an eighteenth-century mind, of the principles of Newtonian mechanics with the necessary assumptions of all human understanding. This led him to the conclusion that while reason can operate outside the confines of scientific "experience," in ethics, art, and religion, it can not there achieve "knowledge," but only "regulative principles." Religion in particular, he agrees with Hume, is founded on faith. But he insists it can be a rational faith, in which reason operates "transcendentally," if not "constitutively" to produce "truth."

For the great majority during the Romantic reaction, the failure of rational religion was reflected in the revivals of traditional religious faith: German Pietism, English Evangelicalism, the great rebirth of Catholicism on the continent. But thoughful men were not satisfied merely to turn back to tradition. If natural theology, operating with the reason and the extrapolated concepts of natural science, was after the analyses of Hume and Kant no longer a tenable enterprise, then the reflective must work out a new kind of rational theology based on a more adequate idea of reason. They were driven on to a fresh analysis of human experience, and a new interpretation of the nature of religion that would not identify it with a set of pseudoscientific propositions that could not even maintain themselves to reason. Religion was not knowledge, but men could gain knowledge of what religion is.

In turning from the abstractions of Newtonian reason to their immediate experience, to their activities as lived, men can certainly find the "reality" of religion, as of so much else. But they can understand that reality only by intellectual methods, by reflective experience. The appeal to experience in criticism of the inadequate Newtonian scheme of understanding could not rest with the bare facts not understood, with life as lived, not even with the religious life immediately enjoyed. It had to go on to new and richer schemes of understanding. The upshot of the Romantic reaction against the Newtonian ideal and its too narrow intellectual method was not, of course, the abandonment of science, but rather the working out of the great enterprise of nineteenth-century experimental science, with its "hypothetical-deductive experimental method." And for those fundamentally interested in the religious life, the rejection of the "scientific religion" of the Age of Reason was not the giving up of all reflection and "reasoning" about religion, but rather the formulation of carefully considered new interpretations which brought new intellectual methods to bear on the facts of concrete religious experience.

The reaction against the misuse of Newtonian ideas was strong. At first, these new interpretations, these new "rational theologies," tended to dismiss "mere science" as irrelevant to their concerns. They took the form of what we conventionally call the "idealistic" philosophies in terms of which men tried to understand and construe and analyze their Romantic experience. "Philosophic reason" and intellectual method was at the outset sharply contrasted with the method of natural science. But as the century wore on, as the sciences of man and of human culture grew in power and adequacy, and became less and less travesties to be escaped from by the sensitive, these philosophic interpretations lost their initial hostility to "science" and drew closer and closer to the more adequate scientific analyses of man's cultural experience. With the emergence of evolutionary psychology, anthropology and sociology, philosophical idealism began to coalesce with this maturing social science. In taking "Religion and Human Experience" as the general theme of this chapter, we are thus directing ourselves toward all that men have found out about religion since Kant and the Romantic idealisms, first in the great Romantic philosophic interpretations of men's religious experience, and then in the emerging scientific study, by methods that are fundamentally extensions of the general methods of natural science, of these same essential facts.

Some philosophical idealists were mere apologists for traditional faith. F. H. Jacobi appealed to pure "faith," *Glaube,* exalting it above Newtonian reason. Later, he called this religious faith "Reason," *Vernunft,* distinguishing it sharply from mere scientific "understanding," *Verstand.* This distinction was popularized in English by Coleridge and Emerson, who stand closest to Jacobi among the Germans. Hamann, the "Wizard of the North," went through Enlightenment rationalism, saw the collapse of rational religion, and fell back on the Lutheran faith of his childhood. Schelling ultimately aligned himself, though with what today would be called elaborate "existentialist" overtones, with the Catholic tradition.

But other idealists felt that to be tenable, the traditional religious world-view must be profoundly reinterpreted and reconstructed; and these men became the religious Liberals, Modernists, or Radicals. Hence the very Romantic reaction against the scientific ideal that for the great majority meant the rejection of the "modern world," meant, for certain outstanding intellectual leaders, a new venture at assimilation, at "modernism," far richer and more sensitive than the eighteenth-century rational religion.

Thus it is not only present-day orthodoxy that goes back to the Romantic religious revivals for its immediate inspiration. The religious "Liberalism" and "Modernism" of the last century and a half owes its strength and its intellectual formulations to that same reaction against rationalism, and to the religious leaders and philosophers who then tried to reconstruct Christianity. That, in fact, is just the trouble with the "liberal"

Protestantism of the past century: intellectually and philosophically it has been a hundred years out of date. It was continuing to revolt against Newtonian science, in its nineteenth-century forms, still seeking a realm of religious truth inaccessible to scientific inquiry, at the very time that an enlarged scientific method and concepts were making such an escape both unnecessary and futile.

This is the trouble also with that form of religious "modernism" called "Neo-Orthodoxy." This further venture at modernism and assimilation has brought its conception of human nature up to date, to express our current mood of disillusionment and to suit the fashionable contemporary temper of our Age of Anxiety; hence at the moment it seems to be enjoying a *succès d'estime.* Whether such an obviously emotional reaction against nineteenth-century self-confidence has really escaped the historical relativities of the day is more doubtful. Disillusionment bred of revulsion from former illusions is hardly the best evidence of objective truth. But to express these strictly modern values, the new Gospel of Sin has reverted to idealistic philosophies which are the very quintessence of the Romantic pessimism and *Weltschmerz* of a century ago, philosophies rooted in an ultimate Romantic voluntarism and irrationalism, both intellectual and practical. If they are resolved to be "contemporary" and "up to date" at all costs, the Neo-Orthodox might at least set forth their contemporary moral values through a philosophy which also embodies and expresses contemporary intellectual values.

The original thinkers among the religious idealists were all Germans: the nineteenth-century English and American thinkers took over the German ideas at second hand, in diluted, desultory, and fragmentary form. They are all echoes of their German sources: in England, Coleridge, Carlyle, Matthew Arnold and the Broad Churchmen, and the later English Idealists, T. H. Green, Benjamin Jowett, John and Edward Caird. In America, the New England Unitarians, notably Emerson and Theodore

Parker, introduced German "Transcendentalism." Outside New England, religious liberalism and idealism were felt in America much later than in Europe, in the eighties and nineties, and then largely at third hand, in dependence on English dependents of the Germans. Here belong Lyman Abbott, Washington Gladden, Henry Churchill King, Borden P. Bowne; only Josiah Royce rose to a direct acquaintance with the German sources, and taught scores of Harvard students how to sublimate Calvinism into the "genteel tradition" of religious idealism.

But the great German religious philosophers entered on a process of reinterpreting the nature and function of religion itself that carried them far toward reconciliation with the later naturalism and experimentalism of the more scientific philosophies of the new century. Though they often failed to realize it, they adopted an attitude that ultimately transformed the problem of defending a religious interpretation of the world into that of developing a philosophy of religion that would need no "defense" against scientific knowledge and methods. There is a direct growth from the great Romantic religious philosophies to our own present-day naturalistic and humanistic interpretations of religion. The German pioneers showed the way to our own insistence on the values and the reality of the religious life without literal belief in its myths. They are hence fundamentally important for our own reconciliation of religion with knowledge. There has been a direct development from their thought to the present-day views that religion is a poetic and imaginative celebration of life, or a consecration to a prophetic clarification of the values of social idealism. The more recent discovery that religion is really a nonprofessional form of psychotherapy is the outcome of a later wave of German Romantic psychology.

Three major interpretations of religion were offered by the Romantic idealists. The first is that religion is a form of knowledge, a philosophical interpretation and explanation of the universe, using symbols where pure philosophy uses only concepts.

The content and aim of religion and philosophy are the same. This view is a continuation of the eighteenth-century conception of religion as a matter of intellectual beliefs, a renewed emphasis on the explanatory function of religion. It is rational religion with a reconstructed and perhaps more adequate conception of reason.

It is inevitable, when science is pushing religion hard, to claim that religion can overcome science on the latter's own ground, that it can give a more adequate explanation of experience. The great religious problem of the nineteenth century was the conflict with and the ultimate adjustment to science: it was primarily intellectual and theological. Hence inevitably it made theology seem central in the religious life. This view has become deeply engrained in the popular mind, though it is now refuted by every disinterested study of the religious life, anthropological, psychological, and historical; and certainly the most momentous changes in religion in the nineteenth century have scarcely turned out to be in beliefs, in theology.

The result of this view is, first, if religion and philosophy are identical, then philosophy is committed to a religious world-view. Philosophy will then be alienated from science, to the great harm of both; the two are still suffering from their mutual suspicions. This is doubly true of a naturalistic social faith, like dialectical materialism. Secondly, if religion be primarily a matter of belief, whenever new knowledge forces a modification of beliefs, the process is all the more disruptive for the religious life. To make belief and knowledge central in religion necessitates constant and unremitting revision.

The great exponent of rationalism in religion, as in all other fields, on the basis of a thoroughly reconstructed conception of reason, was Hegel. Hegel made Christianity into the symbolic expression of his own Absolute Idealism. He had a fine scorn for those Romanticists who took feeling as the basis of the religious life and insight. If this be so, he said of Schleiermacher,

then the dumb adoration of the dog for his master is the highest type of religion.²

For Hegel, religion is the intellectual relation of the finite spirit to the Infinite Spirit. At its highest, religion means to know God, not merely to feel him, or to do his will, though these two are included. Hence Christian love must be intelligent. The most specifically Christian doctrine, the Incarnation, means the complete union between human reason and the World Reason. Man's reason is the Divine element in human nature: it is God coming to self-consciousness in man's knowledge. In other words, it is Intelligence that is God: the rational structure of the universe, realizing itself in human institutions, first becomes conscious of itself in man. "God is Love" is for Hegel the symbol for his dialectic, unfolding and reuniting in sublimated form.

The Incarnation of Reason in Christ is the symbol of the fact that every human reason is a manifestation of the rational structure of the universe, first becoming truly Divine, fully God, in the mind of man. The structure of the world-process becomes God only when it has achieved self-consciousness in man, only when man recognizes himself as a part of it. There can thus be no God without man, without a rationally ordered human society, for Hegel has a thoroughly socialized conception of man and of human experience. For God to be, there must be a Divine, a rational social order. There can be no truly Christian Church, unless it succeeds in establishing a truly Christian society, one that realizes all its rational possibilities. Salvation is hence not the salvation of the individual from the world, but the salvation of the world, of society, from irrationality: the establishment of the Kingdom of God or Reason on earth. It is clear how this Hegelian view became the great inspiration of the Social Gospel. Hegel really understood the

² Hegel had a genuine flair for the comic spirit. He would have appreciated the parody of the table of contents of the Readers Digest that appeared in Punch during 1956, in which one of the titles ran: "My Dog Taught me How to Pray."

Trinity, and the great Alexandrian Greek Doctors. He had little use for Augustine or the Latins, a judgment shared by nearly all the idealistic modernists.

The Hegelian philosophy of religion naturally appealed to those with a strong intellectual interest. And Hegelian idealism was widely taught, especially in Protestant circles outside Germany, as the most promising religious apologetic in the scientific world, and the great instrument for reconstructing Christianity intellectually to incorporate the nineteenth-century humanitarian values. It was Christianity in pure form. In England it became in the seventies the Oxford tradition. Through it English clergymen were taught how to be Christian, though cultured. It is still strong in the protests of older Oxonians against the new Oxford analysis. In America, Hegelianism was the philosophy introduced into the colleges during the nineties to save the students' faith. The President, who was still in those days a scholar, usually taught idealism to the senior class. Hegelianism became entrenched in the more intellectual theological seminaries. It is still strong in denominational colleges which concentrate on a sound idealism and a winning football team.

Hegel's philosophy of religion presented certain difficulties. If religion is Hegelian idealism, and you then abandon idealism, as scientific thought was forcing reflective men to do, even Oxonians and Princeton men, then religion is in a bad way. But even more serious was the fact that a disinterested working out of the logic of Absolute Idealism deprives it of all apologetic or religious value. In the hands of a pure thinker like F. H. Bradley, the Oxford anticlerical, the Absolute is no longer God, beyond good and evil, beyond truth and error, a purely intellectual ideal of perfect knowledge. There is no place left for personal immortality—personality itself ceases to be an ultimate reality—and Bradley was first a sceptic, and then an instrumentalist, in religion as in everything else. McTaggart, the Cambridge Hegelian, likewise stood for an "idealistic atheism." The other two Romantic interpretations of religion thus

proved ultimately more successful. They were not committed to philosophical idealism, though they were first formulated by the Romanticists in its terms. The Hegelian philosophy of religion, in fact, was an attempt at a new "rational theology." It escaped the criticisms leveled by Hume and Kant against natural theology—that nothing of religious value can be gotten out of Newtonian physics, that nothing in mechanics is "Divine."— by constructing a new reason and a new science, a new scheme of intelligibility that did include man and explain his values, and hence could serve as the basis for another rational theology. Our present-day philosophies of nature likewise include man and human values, and hence have also stimulated new natural theologies, in Alexander, Whitehead, Boodin, and Hartshorne. But neither Hegel, nor our contemporary natural theologians, manage to escape the second major criticism of Hume and Kant, that it is impossible rationally to establish any "ground" of experience, any "Absolute" or "Unconditioned."

The two other Romantic interpretations do not identify religion with theology or doctrine at all. They see the function of theology, of religious beliefs, of knowledge itself in the religious life, to be to serve as symbols, not of concepts, not of knowledge, not of anything cognitive, but of feelings and attitudes, or of values and commitments. This is a fundamentally new orientation, to which the classic critiques of the empiricists and of Kant are quite irrelevant. Religion, not being a way of knowing at all, cannot compete with knowledge; but neither can any new knowledge conflict with it.

The second Romantic philosophy of religion holds that religion is not a form of knowledge, but basically a form of art and aesthetic experience. It is a certain organized life of the feelings, a matter of emotion, not of explanation or thinking. It is an aesthetic experience with the whole universe as its object. Theology furnishes symbols, not for the explanatory concepts of science and philosophy, but for man's deepest feelings. This view was worked out by Herder, and more fully by

Schleiermacher. Though developed originally within an idealistic framework, it is quite compatible with a naturalistic metaphysics. And though Schleiermacher's formulation has been
long superseded, it remains one of the strongest tendencies in
liberal religion today.

Schleiermacher is, with Ritschl, one of the two greatest
Protestant theologians of the nineteenth century. He had tremendous influence, which reached the United States through a
host of intermediaries. His spirit is still strong in liberal and
radical religious circles, even though his own formulations have
been long superseded. In his *Reden über die Religion an die
Gebildeten unter ihren Verächtern* (Addresses on religion, to
the cultured among those who despise it) written in the heyday
of Romantic feeling, in 1799, he held that Romantic aesthetic
openness to the universe *is* religion, which is hence a branch of
aesthetics, a form of cosmic consciousness. Truth and falsity
are quite irrelevant to the religious life. Religion is the immediate experience of life, the feeling of its values, the mystic
awareness of life itself. The aesthetic values of living are a revelation of the Divinity in the processes of the world. There is nothing supernatural in religion: the Divine is wholly immanent in
the world, as a distinctive dimension of experience. Divinity
is everywhere: the awareness of it is revelation. The world and
man form one whole, the Absolute. They indeed exist separately,
but in every impression the world makes on men, they become
one with the universe.

Religious experience, the "religious consciousness" (*das
religiöse Bewusstsein*) is a consciousness of the "Absolute,"
that is, of man's oneness with the world. It is a matter of feeling, not of knowledge at all. Schleiermacher disliked intensely
the traditional Platonic "noetic" mysticism, which professed to
furnish "knowledge" of God. He insisted, as against Jacobi and
his "intuitive" faith or "Reason," that no knowledge is to be
found in immediacy. Religion is an independent form of experience, neither morality nor dogmatism and belief. It is an

aesthetic organization of life, although we cannot advance to moral action or to science without such religious feeling for the world. Religion is what Santayana, who stands basically in the tradition of Schleiermacher—though he despised all Romantic feeling, despite his early and controlling interest in Schopenhauer —calls "Piety toward the sources of our being."

In his great theological work, *The Christian Faith,* written in 1817, when the Reaction had hardened the earlier fluid Romantic feeling, Schleiermacher is the first to make central "religious experience," rather than God. Theology is a descriptive science, giving a set of symbols for "religious experience"; the Bible and the various creeds are a record of men's religious experience. Hence no theology can claim a universal or objective validity. All theologies must be reinterpreted in the light of man's growing religious experience. Churches should be free associations of those who have had the same religious experience. They exist, after all, only to foster our human experience of "oneness" with Nature and with Mankind, to stimulate "God-consciousness," the "Kingdom of God."

"Religious experience" Schleiermacher defines as a consciousness and feeling of "absolute dependence" on Nature (*schlechthinniges Abhängigkeitsgefühl*) symbolized as the "will of God," piety toward the sources of our being. Nature is described literally in physics, but it is symbolized as "God," the "Creator," "Providence." The specifically "Christian" experience is the sense of the power of Christian love, the "Living Christ." Whether Jesus ever lived or not is quite immaterial. In fellowship with men in whom such Love is a living reality, we can experience that "Love" ourselves. And in feeling it, we become "one with God," that is, with the Nature of which we are a part, and with all men, in whom Nature is revealed in its highest possibilities.

Jesus had this "God-consciousness" of "oneness" with the universe so clearly that he can mediate it to us. This constitutes his "Divinity." When in fellowship with others we experience "fellowship with Christ," the power of Christian love, and share his sense of oneness with the universe, we share in "Eternal Life," which is not continued existence after death—Schleiermacher rejected personal survival—but "being One" with the Eternal in temporal existence.

Schleiermacher came from the *Herrnhüter,* the Moravian Brethren or German Quakers; and his intellectual power is suffused with the sincerity and attractiveness of the Quaker faith—which almost tempts one to join the Christians.

The third Romantic philosophy of religion holds that religion is not a form of knowledge, as Hegel thought, nor of aesthetic feeling, as Schleiermacher taught, but a form of action, of behavior. The religious life is a life of moral striving, to realize human and social ideals. It is "morality touched with emotion," in the phrase of Matthew Arnold; it is making the "will of God" prevail, building the "Kingdom of Heaven" on earth. "God" is the will you make prevail; "Heaven" is the "Kingdom" you build. This is the ethical interpretation of religion, the "Social Gospel." Many Germans, including Kant himself, and most notably Fichte, worked out its outlines. Albrecht Ritschl [3] is the greatest theological formulator of this position. Like the aesthetic gospel, it too is quite compatible with a naturalistic metaphysics. In Ritschl, Kantianism is pushed further in a pragmatic direction. Hence during the later nineteenth century his philosophical theology became increasingly popular: by 1900 it had come to dominate Protestant liberal theology. It was a theology of social control, to fit the gospel of social justice.

For Ritschl, theology is not metaphysics or ontology: it does not deal with the nature of the world, or "reality." It

[3] Paul Tillich comments: "You put Ritschl into the romantic development. This seems to me entirely impossible. Ritschl was a very sober rationalistic and moralistic follower of Kant, rejecting everything mystical and romantic as strongly as possible. This is the reason I never liked him."

I should not dream of denying any of these statements about Ritschl, especially the last. Mr. Tillich restricts the term "Romantic" in the German fashion. For my own usage, see note 1 on page 76.

deals with "values." It is an affair, not of "judgments of fact," but of "value judgments." This Kantian dichotomy Ritschl made central; it has outlasted his own fame.

For Ritschl, religion springs from the relation of man to the world, not to "God." Man finds himself a part of the world, but he also finds he is able to rise above the world and control it. The religious problem is to win victory over the world, to build the "Kingdom of God," to establish the "reign of righteousness" among men. To achieve this moral end, man needs a higher religious principle to set over against the world, he needs God. In oneness with this Divine principle, man can conquer and control the world. Ritschl is a strong ethical dualist: he sees a great gap between the actual and the ideal. "God" is an hypothesis that can be verified in our lives if we use faith in God to serve our moral ends.

Christ won the true victory, moral victory over the world. He has thus revealed the "will of God," the moral ideal: the reign of righteousness among men, the "Kingdom." We too can win by sharing this ideal, by working for the Kingdom. Christianity is a valid faith, for we can prove that it works: Love can establish the Kingdom. Experience thus confirms the faith of the Christian.

Christ is Divine, because his purpose is Divine. The Virgin Birth, and all other doctrines of Christ's "substance," are all irrelevant. To be "Divine" is to share the Divine purpose; it is not a matter of Christ's "substance" at all. The Trinity, naturally, is quite meaningless for Ritschl. It is much higher to share the Divine purpose than to participate in any supposed "Divine substance."

Christianity is following the "teachings of Christ." We believe in God because we learn that Christ's teachings work: to believe in a God of Love does succeed in transforming the world. "God" means just this power of a moral ideal to realize itself through human striving. "Immortality" is a certain quality of living—Ritschl is agnostic on personal survival after death. The Church is the body of those who are working to bring about the Kingdom of God. Communion with God, prayer, is making the Divine purpose your own, acting for the ideal. Ritschl, like the later Neo-Orthodox, hated quietism or mysticism of any sort.

It is easy to see how a famous Ritschlian teaching in one of our liberal seminaries could say, "I believe in Christ just because I am an atheist"; his successor has put it, "Belief in the *existence* of God is the worst form of atheism." The leaders of liberal religion in America even a generation ago were clear-headed fellows. Their hearts were in the right place—even if they did, and still do, have to take the Christian myths and symbols pretty seriously. At least they have not taken them too literally.

These three Romantic philosophical interpretations of religion represent the three essential tendencies in the religious tradition, which has satisfied intellectual needs, in expressing the meaning of life; aesthetic needs, in expressing the beauties and feelings of life; and ethical needs, in expressing the ends and ideals of life. Any one, taken alone, insofar as it tries to minimize the two others, is doubtless an improverishment of the religious life. Certainly all three have been united and fused in the great religions.

So long as men could believe in philosophical idealism, Hegel's religious rationalism proved the most popular. With the emergence of scientific naturalisms, the views of Schleiermacher and Ritschl have come to the fore as the chief contemporary tendencies in the philosophy of religion, joined more recently by the conviction of our Age of Anxiety that religion is primarily a personal psychotherapeutics. Aesthetic religion and ethical religion are our heritage from the Romantics. Ethical naturalism appeals to Protestants and to Jews as they grow doubtful of God, and fall back on the moral will and the stern drive for social justice. Aesthetic naturalism appeals rather to Catholics and Anglo-Catholics, who fall back on the poetic and artistic symbolism of religion. There is an emphasis on the aesthetic appreciation of the values of life, and an emphasis on the moral impulse to extend those values to all men. It is the old antithesis between the priest and the prophet, between ritual worship and making the world new, between religion as a means of feeling good inside and as a means of transforming society, between personal consolation and social justice, between the beautiful ritual and the social settlement or the moral crusade.

For both older conceptions, as well as for their younger sister therapy, theology, the intellectual element, has been pushed into the background, and a general naturalistic faith more or less accepted. Theology at best, it is held, furnishes symbols for aesthetic feelings or for moral ideals. The long effort at intellectual reconciliation with science, if not exactly a failure, has at least come to seem irrelevant. There is "no real conflict" between religion and science, though it is too hard to explain just how. It is fashionable to be impatient of all theology: religion is life, not idle speculation. What is important is the moral teaching of Christ—or of Paul, if he seems more up to date—not the curious theology of his atonement. Let men believe as they please, but unite in terms of symbolic worship, to make effective social and moral ideals. What men think about God is really of very little import, as long as they practice their religion.

These are the real religious faiths of today: the faith in feeling and beauty, the faith in social justice, and the lesser faith in pastoral therapeutics and confident living. The genuine religious problem is how to reconcile them. For the intelligent, the conflict of religion and science is no longer a vital problem: they have abandoned any attempt to find knowledge in religion. But there is a real conflict, running through our entire lives, between the religion of beauty, the religion of ethics, and the religion of healing. The greatness of past religions lay in combining these three faiths; their weakness, in claiming to give an independent explanation of the universe also. It is easy to see that all three are essential: without an appreciation of values, it is futile to work to extend them; and unless we are willing to create them and spread them, it is ignoble to live in parasitic enjoyment. Our religious life seems split into an unimaginative social reform, a callous aestheticism, and an ill-informed ministering to minds diseased. It would be hard to say which is the more dubious, the routine settlement work, the choir-singing in St. Midas's on Fifth Avenue, or the popular uplift psychology of best-selling prima donnas of the pulpit. Perhaps the religious life needs a little intelligence. Possibly there is some place left for knowledge in it after all.

Can that place be the one assigned to "spiritual" knowledge by the idealistic philosophies deriving from the Romantic era? In their revolt against the Newtonian world, these philosophies were quite content to leave to physical science and its methods the entire realm of mere "nature" in which it had triumphed. Their claim was that man and his ideal interests, morality, art, and religion, belong to a different "dimension" or "realm" of the universe, to which is appropriate a very different kind of knowledge, operating by quite different and non-scientific intellectual methods. Religious knowledge in particular deals with a higher realm inaccessible to the mere understanding and its plodding methods, a realm of "freedom," or a "transcendental" realm, the idealists usually put it. Hegel's "philosophic knowledge," for whose concepts religion employs symbols, is sharply distinguished from the scientific knowledge of nature. Ritschl's "value-judgments," the only kind possible in religion, as in ethics and aesthetics, are set over against all theoretical or factual judgments, which belong to science. "God is the Absolute," is a theoretical judgment; "God is a Father," a value-judgment. Theoretical judgments state the objective nature of a thing; value-judgments, its value to us. Value-judgments, Ritschl held, are as certain as scientific judgments, but not necessarily of universal validity. Even Schleiermacher's "religious knowledge," as the description of the "religious consciousness," is quite different from scientific knowledge. Thus it is characteristic of all three religious formulations of philosophic idealism to assign to the knowledge that has a place in religion a distinctive and unique character and status. For all three, religious knowledge, if not in the conventional sense "supernatural," is at least "extranatural."

The concern with "religious experience," developing out of Schleiermacher's interpretation of the "religious consciousness" and powerfully reinforced by later psychological analyses like James's *Varieties of Religious Experience,* has tended more and more to conceive that "experience" as itself quite unique, with a distinctive object of its own. Many idealists and later philosophic thinkers have followed William James in making central to religion the mystic experience. Rudolf Otto has identified the peculiar quality to which the religious experience is directed with the "Numinous" or the "Holy." And present-day Kierkegaardian religious Existentialism has contrasted strongly the religious knowledge given in practical or "existential judgments" with theoretical or scientific knowledge. "Existential knowledge," it is held, is "participating knowledge," not detached, objective knowledge: it involves a practical or "existential" commitment to its object. This Kierkegaardian conception, consecrated by the Existentialists, is apt to strike Americans as rather fancy language for James's "will to believe," which he justified in cases of "live options" that cannot be decided on grounds of public evidence. But such choices James at least did not identify with "knowledge."

In all these and in other ways, since the Romantic reaction sympathetic students of religion have tried to distinguish "religious knowledge" sharply from scientific knowledge, so that there will be no competition between the two, above all so that scientific analyses and criticisms, if directed against religious claims, will seem to be irrelevant and out of place. Now, it is true that all these experienced qualities, feelings, and attitudes are doubtless genuine and "real" enough: they are clearly enjoyed and entertained, by many at least, who are sincerely convinced that through them they have learned essential "truths."

But as in the case of all forms of nonreflective experience, it is doubtful whether of themselves, considered as self-contained, uncriticized "immediate experiences," they can rightly be said to furnish "knowledge," except the sheer encountering itself, what has been called "knowledge by acquaintance." Clearly, they do not proclaim by their mere occurrence how they are related to other experiences, or, what is crucial, how their supposed "objects" are connected with other experienced objects. They do not come to us uttering clearly their causes, conditions, and consequences. All these matters are obviously occasions that call for the kind of critical intellectual inquiry we call "scientific." And the human and cultural sciences that have been for a century concerned to analyze these important aspects and relations of experience, psychology, anthropology, sociology, and the rest, have devoted long attention to these very questions, and have by now amassed extensive knowledge about them. "Immediate experience" is not itself knowledge. For as Santayana says, "Knowledge is not like digestion, and we do not devour what we mean." Immediate experience does indeed furnish indispensable and essential subject matter to be understood. But however great its value, immediate experience is not, in the light of present-day philosophy or science, itself a way of understanding.

It is just this mass of scientific knowledge now acquired about religion that has thrown most light on the role of knowledge in religion. This understanding has played a major part in the abandonment in our generation of the nineteenth-century prejudice that belief and theology form the central features of the religious life. As we started by pointing out, the most revolutionary effect of science upon religion springs not from newer views of the world and of man, but from newer views of religion—of the nature and function of religion itself. Whatever "conflict" between science and religion is still left today arises from the clash between scientific and traditional views of the character of religion.

The impact of evolutionary psychology on the understanding of men's religious experience was tremendous. It has here been barely suggested. Still more revolutionary has been the force of the more recent depth psychology in altering men's notions of the source and the functioning of religious beliefs. The tendency here has been to interpret the whole intellectual side of religion, the entire body of religious ideas, as springing from a subconscious motivation. Religious beliefs have been taken as essentially wish projections, emotional symbols; Freud even went so far as to call them "illusions." Something of this reorientation can be gained from the thoughtful and moderate recent book of Erwin R. Goodenough, professor of the history of religion at Yale, *Toward a Mature Faith*. Among depth psychologists, Jung has proved much more sensitive and imaginative in dealing with religious symbols than Freud, as well as less hostile to religion in general, and his speculative hypotheses about the collective and universal nature of such symbols are much richer and more suggestive than Freud's. Hence it is Jung who has proved the most influential in the reconstruction of the conceptions of the sources and functions of religious symbolism.

It is, however, not the psychologists but the anthropologists, the sociologists, and the historians of religion who have carried furthest the reinterpretation of the nature and function of religious activities and practices. They have been much less provincial than the psychologists, who until recently have displayed the tendency to restrict themselves to the bourgeois Western culture of Vienna of the early nineteen hundreds. Above all, they have viewed religion as part of a group culture, and not as a private "experience"—or neurosis—taken in splendid isolation. They have seen and analysed religious activity as a whole. Even the best psychologists, like the pioneering James, have merely examined certain selected "psychological" aspects of the religious life. Protestant psychologists in particular long tended to concentrate on the evangelical crises of religious experience.

And the psychologists have notoriously been much more speculative and much less scientific and objectively critical in their methods and hypotheses than the anthropologists—than those of the Boas school at least.

As a result of all this sustained analysis of man's cultural experience, it has become clear that religion has never existed apart from the rest of men's living. Religious activities have been an organized expression of the feelings, actions, and beliefs of men, centering around the emotionally significant and valuable elements of their social experience. They can express whatever men have deeply felt, in appropriately institutionalized forms. Religious practices have thus celebrated and consecrated men's normal social activities, as in the great agricultural festivals marking the turning points of the farmer's calendar. They have also given expression to men's emotions of need and uncertainty in the face of the extraordinary and mysterious, the fearsome crises of living.

In simpler societies, the religious life has consisted primarily of ritual acts, of doing something together with one's fellows with deep and shared feeling. The very doing seems to help. Such intensely felt action evokes its own objects. Myths took form and crystalized; belief in supernatural powers, and finally in "gods," was born. The desire for more order, when present, created pantheons. Peoples like the Greeks or the Hindus felt the impulse to intellectual harmony, and approached the notion of one all-controlling Divine power. The Hebrews generalized their tribal tabus into a legal monotheism.

These ways of ritual acting themselves had consequences. They integrated and unified the groups that practiced them, into a cooperative human complex, into a tribe, a city-state, a kingdom, a people. They helped that people to be conscious of themselves as a group, to work and live together. They generated common loyalties and ties, a common experience, a common world of the imagination, a common vision of the values to be attained in living. Even in their crudest form, they made it possible for that group to be a group, to survive in a hostile world. This fostering a common awareness and purpose is served by religious "celebration" and "consecration," and persists as a fundamental function of all religious activity.

As civilizations developed, religious activities came, with increasing curiosity and deepened and broadened moral insights, to express intellectual and moral values. Myths were turned into explanations of the striking features of life and of its scene: they appeared now as answers to questions, and developed into a kind of speculative science. Rites, myths, and magic took on a moral significance: they became symbols of moral customs and ideals. Reformers and prophets arose, to remold the old ideas and ways of acting the better to meet these intellectual and moral demands. They in turn faded into the realm of myth and magic; rites gathered about their memory. Sacred books set down the customs and rituals, the messages of the prophets, the aspirations of the more imaginative leaders. The great civilizations developed complex religious institutions with elaborate lore, magnificent rites and techniques. Along with ancient spells and ritual, sacrifices, prayers, and techniques of worship, they came also to embody the successive insights of spiritual geniuses.

Religion has thus been primarily an organized expression of men's emotions and conduct. It has been a way of shared feeling and acting in the face of the most important concerns of living. In societies that have generated an intellectual interest, it has also been a way of believing and even thinking; but, with few exceptions, systematic belief has been a secondary and derived matter. Religion was a social force before the gods were born; it has persisted as a spiritual power in cultures like India and China and Greece where the gods have given way to other and less personal interpretations of the Divine.

To show how far scholarly students of men's religious institutions have now come from taking religious beliefs literally, from taking "truth" and "knowledge" as the essence of the faiths by which men live, I can hardly do better than quote from the historian of religion already mentioned, Goodenough: "We accept the projected fantasies of others not only in the form of poetry, painting, and the novel. We accept similar projections in religion. . . . Gradually the dreams of much of eastern Asia have come to settle in the highly complex figure of Buddha, as Jewish civilization centered in Jahweh, and Christian civilizations in Christ and Mary. Into these figures, and many more like them all over the world, have been packed the dreams and wishes of the peoples of these civilizations. The great religious teachers have been people who projected ideas and figures of the kind that answered the needs of their culture. . . . The teachings of the great leaders in religion have endured simply on the pragmatic basis that they, in contrast to the others, projected dreams of God and of right, of the way to spiritual (and physical) security, which really helped the men who accepted them.

"Why do I call these teachings about God and the gods wish projections? . . . No one would have any hesitation in describing figures such as the gods of ancient Egypt and Mesopotamia and Greece and Phoenicia, and Persia and China, to say nothing of the gods of savages, as wish projections. . . . Good or bad, kind or ferocious, we recognize all these gods as wish projections—all except our own. But should we, can we, make that exception? I do not think we can. Whether men justify their projection by arguments about the nature of the Infinite and the Absolute, or just believe in God as they have learned about him as children, he still seems to me to be as much a projection in our civilization as among the Aztecs or the Eskimos. This means not that there is no God, but only that all human notions of him are projections. That is why I reject so sharply Freud's term 'illusion,' which he used for traditional religions, especially Judaism and Christianity. For there is a large measure of truth in many of our projections, while 'illusions' implies, like a mirage, that we are experiencing things which do not exist at all except in our own desires. . . .

"We must, I saw, recognize that man lives not by his knowledge of right, truth, meaning, and the like, but, basically ignorant of life, by his refusing to believe that life is meaningless even though he does not understand it, and by his projecting a meaning and pattern upon it. This discovery was to me not paralyzing at all. . . . For if man has always lived on projections he can continue to do so. The trouble is not that our stabilizing ideas and deities are projections, but that we are becoming too self-conscious, too superior in the bad sense of the term, to be ourselves and go on projecting." [4]

The precise function Goodenough assigns to religious beliefs is strongly colored by his predominantly Jungian psychology, and would hardly be universally accepted. But his general view, that religious beliefs and ideas are not knowledge but "symbols," that they cannot be taken as literally "true," but that "there is a large measure of truth in many of" them—this view would be widely entertained today by most thoughtful students of religion. It of course leaves the crucial question unanswered: Just what precisely constitutes the "large measure of truth" in religious symbols? That is why the analysis of the nature and function of such symbols occupies so central a place in the philosophical interpretation of religion today, and why we shall have to give it careful attention in our concluding analysis. For the problem has today become for thoughtful religious men what it became long ago in Greece and in India: How can we live the religious life when for us its myths have been "broken," when we recognize that its beliefs and ideas cannot be taken as literally "true"?

Goodenough's primarily Jungian interpretation, we have said, would not be widely accepted. Indeed, there is as yet no complete agreement, in spite of the long study devoted to the problem, about the nature and function of religion in human cultural experience. For religion is still usually treated as a term to be defined, rather than as a concrete subject matter to

---

[4] From *Toward a Mature Faith,* by Erwin R. Goodenough, © 1955 by Prentice-Hall, Inc., published by Prentice-Hall, Inc., Englewood Cliffs, New Jersey.

be investigated and analyzed. The attempt to define the function of religion is notoriously complex and difficult; it has never been satisfactorily carried out. It is obviously an empirical inquiry. It involves starting with a function vaguely denoted, exploring a great variety of what we should all agree can be called "religions," and the many different things they do, and then on the basis of a certain number of these functions trying to draw some kind of line. Since all the functions that all religions perform are not performed by any one religion, the "function" of religion is hardly to be identified with any common core of operating. That "function" is rather a complex group of functions, any selection from which can be said to be "religious"—to be "functioning religiously."

Still, to give some indication of the conditions of a preliminary denotation of what is involved in the function of religion—what is involved in "functioning religiously"—since I want to go on to the distinctive functions of knowledge in the religious life, I shall content myself with a very brief statement of the traits that seem to be essential to anything we should be willing to recognize as a "religion."

(1) Something happens to the individual. As John Dewey puts it, he achieves a "unification of the self through allegiance to inclusive ideal ends." [5] As Paul Tillich expresses it, "he is grasped by an ultimate concern." [6] Neither of these formulations is adequate, but they may both together serve to point at least to the personal transformation.

(2) What happens in and to the individual is dependent on and derivative from something ultimately social. It occurs through participation, however personalized the particular form may have become, in an institutionalized social art. The roots of religion are social and cultural, though the flower and the fruit may be something highly individual, and quite unique.

(3) This religious art employs distinctive techniques, pro-

---

[5] John Dewey, *A Common Faith* (1934), p. 33.
[6] Paul Tillich, *Systematic Theology*, I (1951), p. 12.

cedures, and language, and religious myths and symbols that organize, unify, and express social experience, in order to celebrate, consecrate, and clarify social values.

The function of religion thus involves certain consequences for the individual, variously stated in our religious tradition as "salvation," "strengthening faith in God," "practical commitment to an ultimate concern." It involves certain social consequences: the consecration, clarification, and criticism of the values shared by the religious group. And it takes place through religious arts employing certain activities, practices, and techniques, including the mechanism of religious language and symbols, to express, organize, and unify the social experience of the group. These three traits, the function for the individual, the function for the group, and the social techniques, however individualized, seem to be the necessary conditions for the functioning of religion in the fullest sense. In our next chapter we can specify a little more precisely what is involved in "functioning religiously."

In these three functions, just what is the role of knowledge and truth? It is to this question that our last chapter will devote itself.

Chapter Four. *Knowledge, Intelligence, and Religious Symbols*

We are now in a position to ask once more our major question. What, in the light of this long history of relations intimate if not always legitimatized between them, is the rightful place of knowledge in religion? At the outset we can, I think, agree on certain preliminary negative conclusions. Note well this "preliminary": for as we push our exploratory investigation we shall be forced to introduce significant qualifications. But, accepting the main features of the analysis of the institution of religion worked out by our cultural sciences, we can say, religion and knowledge are clearly not rivals for our intellectual respect, though they may well be for our affections. This holds whether that "knowledge" be taken as the deliverances of the enterprise of science, as the findings of the thoughtful philosophical interpretation of experience, or as the opinions of mere sound common sense. These are the three major kinds of formulated assertions or propositions capable of being tested by evidence and of being judged to be true. As thus susceptible to verification, they are commonly agreed to constitute "knowledge"; they include both descriptions of facts and explanations of those facts, for both take the form of statements *that* such and such is the case. This is the sense of "knowledge" whose role in religion we are questioning. It is necessary to be precise about just what we mean by "knowledge," lest our arguments turn into quarrels about the mere use of words. It is beyond doubt, there can be no serious conflict between religion and "knowledge" in this sense, "knowledge" taken as factual descriptions or theoretical explanations of anything, as propositions that are "warrantedly assertible" or "true."

For religion offers no descriptions and no explanations

whatever independent of men's best secular knowledge—though its presence and its challenge may, and historically has, come to influence that knowledge profoundly. Religion is rather itself a human activity that demands careful observation and description, explanation, reflective understanding, and intelligent criticism. A religion, we have seen, may well embrace in the body of beliefs associated with it an explanation, a truth, drawn from some nonreligious source. The religious thought of those interested in explanations normally does, and certainly in the Christian tradition has done so from the beginning. These explanations embodied in religious beliefs then may well come later to conflict with new and better secular explanations: this too has happened again and again, and in some areas of inquiry is still happening today. But the conflict will then arise between different explanations within the common intellectual enterprise of discovering truth. It will not break out between the religious life and fresh explanation or knowledge.

We can assume, therefore, that all religious beliefs without exception are "mythology." That is, they are all religious "symbols." If such symbols can be said to possess any kind of "truth," they certainly do not possess the literal truth of the factual statements of the descriptive sciences or of common sense, or the "warranted assertibility" and explanatory value of the well founded theories of science and philosophy.

In passing, we might well ask, are scientific beliefs, the hypotheses, theories and laws that go beyond mere descriptive statements of fact, any the less "mythological," any the less "symbols" or instruments of the techniques of inquiry? If they too be indeed symbols, then they are symbols of something else, surely, and perhaps in a significantly different way. But the same Goodenough already quoted goes on to insist, rightly enough, that if religious beliefs and symbols are "wish projections," so too are scientific hypotheses and theories. Neither can rightly claim to be literal statements of the nature of things.

To this negative conclusion, that there is no literal description of fact or explanatory truth to be found in religion in general or in Christianity in particular, there would today be widespread agreement. It would be found not only among scientific and philosophic students of religion, but also among the many Christian theologians and philosophers who would not pride themselves on holding to the letter of orthodoxy. The full implications of this position, however, seem not always to be realized. It means, for instance, not only that the "existence of God" is a "myth" or symbol; Neo-Orthodox theologians can easily take this in their stride. It means also that the doctrine of Original Sin is likewise a "myth" or symbol, and supplies no literal truth about man that other adequate analyses of human nature can not and have not been able to arrive at. Between a religious, even a Christian, view of human nature, and a sound psychological analysis, there can be no conflict—as explanations, as truth. In practice this seems a much harder doctrine to take seriously. It is by no means clear that all the Neo-Orthodox would countenance it.

The reason, no doubt, is that adequate analyses of human nature and sound psychological judgments are not easy to come by—as yet. For it is not very difficult to suspect certain limitations in behavioristic psychology. Graham Wallas once remarked that it had gotten along swimmingly as far up the scale as the decorticated white rat; but since then of course it has gone on to Pavlov's dog. Indeed, even Joseph Wood Krutch has a certain justification in his distrust of the adequacy of all laboratory methods to deal with the nature of man. And as for depth psychology, despite the spate of candidates, it has still to give birth to its Newton; as yet we have had only a number of rival Keplers. In this far from stabilized climate of psychological opinion, it is not surprising that genuine insight is still to be won from poets like Paul or Augustine. But poetic insight into human nature, however revealing in particular, is inherently far from exhaustive or balanced. And sensitive religious students of the nature of man might well pause to recollect that if Kierkegaard be an authentic and gifted poet whose insights are to be taken seriously, so too is Jesus of Nazareth.

At the moment, indeed, the severest specific intellectual conflict between newer ideas and the older ones enshrined in religious thought is raised when religious men confront some of our recent psychological theories. It is not the world but the nature of man that so-called "science" today seems to be distorting. Since for all their suggestiveness and their promise that they will lead to future knowledge, these speculative theories and approaches to the analysis of human nature of our psychological Keplers are not notorious for their sobriety, sanity, or general wisdom and judicious appraisals, the religious men who are shocked would do well to exercise a little toleration, and patience. The morrow will bring new theories of man.

We can agree, secondly, that if no truth is to be found in religion that can possibly conflict with the explanations of science, neither does religion furnish men with any *additional* "truth" discoverable by specifically religious methods that will supplement the conclusions of patient inquiry. It provides no further "truth" about the world or man not attainable by the intellectual methods we ordinarily call "scientific." By this time liberal Christians and Jews have pretty well reconstructed their beliefs so that they no longer come into open conflict with any of the verified conclusions of the scientists. But they are still apt to hold that their faith adds further knowledge, either explanations of a realm inaccessible to scientific inquiry, or an additional kind of explanation of the same realm from which that inquiry selects. This assumption is historically a holdover from the days of idealistic philosophy, when the narrow and limited methods and assumptions of natural science were obviously inapplicable to human experience, and hence inevitably drove men on to other methods and assumptions for inquiring into those richer and more concrete fields. The apologetic strategy of these belated idealists is to point to the obvious fact that mathematical and laboratory techniques do not yield significant results when applied to the moral and spiritual activities of men. But these are only the *techniques* and *procedures* of physical science; they are emphatically not "scientific method" and "logic" themselves. Of course practical procedures differ from field to field, but the logic and method of inquiry are the same for all fields, as well as the rules of evidence.

Nor can the view be sustained that "religious experience" is a specific and distinctive cognitive activity of man, involving unique factors or materials, and hence bringing a knowledge of its special objects which is to be gained in no other manner. "Religious experience" is not unique. In this respect it is not like the "mystic experience," so exploited in this century as an apologetic for a distinctive and "higher" religious knowledge. If we take "mystic" as an immediate quality of experience—or as a quality of immediate experience—viewed from the personal side, this unique quality can indeed function religiously, it can indeed play an important part in the religious life. But it is clearly by no means necessary to that life. And it can occur quite apart from the religious situation, as the effect of certain drugs, for example. The specifically religious function of the mystic experience is to strengthen religious commitment, conviction, and vision, but not to give theoretical knowledge, of God or anything else.

"Functioning religiously" is indeed very much like "functioning aesthetically": any set of factors can be involved in the practice of the religious life, in "functioning religiously." Just as no one type of material alone possesses aesthetic qualities or powers, but any type can on occasion function aesthetically, just so, no one type of activity or "experience" alone possesses religious qualities or powers, but any type can on occasion function religiously. The qualities or powers become "religious" in character if they function in the specifically religious way. What such religious functioning involves as its essential components we attempted to characterize briefly at the close of the previous chapter.

Indeed, "mystic experience," or any other similar type of immediate experience, like Otto's experience of "the Holy" or "the Numinous," or like the "Thou" [1] of the "I-Thou experience," while genuine enough, does not and cannot by itself tell us what its object "really is," what its relations are to other objects in experience, what are its causes and conditions, what are its values and consequences. For that we have to turn to intellectual inquiry, to scientific methods.

Again, while "religious experience" can be supremely valuable, it is clearly not an experience of "values" about which we can come to learn in no other way. It can not tell us what those values "are": their nature, their consequences, their relations to their causes and conditions and to other values. Only inquiry can do that. Scientific method and logic can of course deal with values, in answering precisely these questions about them. Indeed, science is essentially a method for the *criticism* of values, for determining which beliefs are *better than* others.

Nor does there seem to be any such thing as "existential truth," quite different from and irrelevant to "nonparticipating detached scientific truth." [2] Devotion—"existential commitment"—to something may bring many fruits: sympathy, understanding of its appeal from within, sensitive feeling, awareness of qualities, and many others. But none of these consequences is "knowledge" or "truth." We cannot indeed become "acquainted with" a painting without looking at it with our eyes. But eyes alone are not sufficient for an understanding of the painting, for knowledge of its aesthetic or other "meaning." Likewise, sharing a belief may be essential to becoming acquainted with what it is—"with what it means," we say. But mere sharing hardly establishes the truth of the belief. Many a German through

---

[1] Martin Buber has made it clear that he does not pretend to know what God or the Divine "really is"—what God may be apart from his relations to man. He reports rather that in his own experience, and in the experience of the Hebrew people he finds recorded in the "Biblical religion" of the Hebrew Scripture, God is always encountered in the guise of a person.

[2] The phrase is Paul Tillich's.

sharing and commitment found "existential truth" in the Nazi ideology. Commitment may be a necessary condition of some kinds of truth, though there is such a thing as imaginative sympathy or empathy. But it is clearly not a sufficient criterion. Here too only patient inquiry and checking will suffice.

Religion, then, furnishes no additional "truth" about the world or man or the Divine. What it does furnish—and here the "extranaturalists" or "transcendentalists" are clearly right—is additional subject matter, experiences and qualities that are found and enjoyed, visions that are seen. Religion gives men more, and how much more only the participant can realize. In this it is like art, which likewise furnishes no supplementary truth, but does open whole worlds to be explored, whole heavens to be enjoyed. What the poet, the artist, the prophet or the saint beholds, is genuine and important enough, if his vision be actually authentic. But visions are not understood by vision. They may not, and perhaps need not, be understood at all, in order to live by them. But if we do seek to understand visions, we can only understand and interpret them by patient inquiry. The intellectual clarification of religious insight and vision is one of the most important of all contributions which intelligence can make to the religious life. It is the essential and necessary condition of the most valuable of all the functions of intelligence in religion, the criticism of the activities and visions of man's spiritual experience of the Divine.

If the function of religious beliefs is not to generate knowledge and truth, what is their function? Very early in every great religious tradition, reflective men came to see that the ordinary ideas entertained and used in worship, prayer and ritual could not be "literally" true. The idea of God, for example, employed by the unreflective in the actual practice of the religious arts, could not be adequate to the true nature of the Divine. God could not be "really" the animal, or natural force, or carved image, the imaginative picture, in which the average man conceives the Divine. He could not be even the highest human image, the "Father," or the kind of "person" who in the present fashion seems appropriately approached in terms of the "I-Thou" experience. Important and even indispensable in religious practice as are these ways of imagining the Divine, they are all, reflective men soon came to realize, attempts to fit the idea of God in somehow with the rest of men's experience. But they are not adequate definitions or descriptions of the religious dimension of that experience. They cannot be taken as literal accounts of the Divine. They are imaginative and figurative ways of conceiving the relations of men and their ideals to the nature of things, and to its religious dimension. We have seen how the Greeks came to this insight, that all ideas of the Divine are necessarily imaginative and symbolic. We have seen how Philo of Alexandria worked out the consequences of this notion for the Hebraic tradition, and how the Alexandrian Doctors and Augustine carried the same realization into Christian theology.

All ideas of God, like all other religious beliefs, are without exception *religious symbols*. This means that they perform what is primarily a religious function. They are employed in religious experience, and serve to carry on the religious life. They are techniques, instruments, in terms of which ritual and the other religious arts are conducted.

But not all conceptions of God are imaginative images drawn from men's experience of their fellows. There is a notorious difference between ideas of God whose primary function is to serve in religious practice, which are employed in the actual conduct of religious techniques, worship, prayer and the rest— ideas like those of God as a loving Father, God as a stern Judge, God as the "Thou" of the "I-Thou" relationship—and a quite different set of ideas of God worked out for very different purposes by philosophic theologians. The function of these latter ideas, as we have seen, is not so much to serve in the practical living of the religious life as to introduce intellectual consistency between the different areas of men's experience. We have examined the long history of this philosophic enterprise in the

Western tradition. Men have tried to elaborate notions of God that would fit in with their own reflective understanding of the world and of their experience. They have tried to find conceptions of the Divine that would construe and interpret religious insight in terms of their particular philosophy and science, and adjust it to the rest of their experience in ways that would be consistent with their other beliefs. We have seen how for the Jews and the Christians rational theology began with the interpretation of the Hebrew and Christian symbols in the light of the Neoplatonic philosophy of the Hellenistic world.

Western philosophic theology has conceived God in terms of the ultimate intellectual ideal enshrined in the successive schemes of understanding, the changing philosophies, our Western culture has developed. In each scheme the highest object of knowledge has been identified with the highest good; and thus has been achieved, for that philosophy, a harmony between men's moral and religious faith and their way of understanding the world, between "faith" and "reason." God, we have seen, has been thus identified successively with the ultimate conception of the Platonic science of the Hellenistic age, the Logos or objective rational structure of the cosmos; with the first principle of the Aristotelian science of the Middle Ages, the ultimate Final Cause or Prime Mover; with the mathematical Order of Nature of Cartesian science; with the original Force or Creator of Newtonian science; with the Absolute or Unconditioned of idealistic philosophy; with the first principle of creative evolution, with Alexander's "nisus toward Deity," or with Whitehead's "principle of concretion", with the *Sein* of Heidegger's existential ontology. The intellectual and religious success of these rational theologies has depended upon the power of the particular scheme of science employed to understand and illuminate man and his various activities and values. The attempts have been least successful when, as with Newtonian science, there was provided no adequate way of understanding human life.

But broadly, experience makes clear that any philosopher

worth his salt can find in the thought of his day such an intellectual symbol for God. Or rather, any philosophy that has not found
such an intellectual symbol for the religious dimension of the
world, for the Divine, is a truncated philosophy—and what such
a "philosophy" is like may be observed in many widely professed
at the present time. But with our deepened knowledge of how
beliefs actually function in religion, we have come to realize today that these successive philosophical ideas of God, though they
have all managed to play a useful and indeed an essential part
in the different schemes of understanding by which men have organized their intellectual experience, are themselves all symbols
too. They are of course quite different from the concrete images
that have been employed in the religious arts, and would hardly
serve in the actual practice of worship or prayer. Despite the
apocryphal story, it is doubtful whether even a disciple of Wieman
ever really prayed to the principle of concretion. Such ideas are
intellectual symbols rather than symbols of religious practice.
They have a religious function only in the lives of those who must
understand. Only the Gods of metaphysicians are metaphysical
principles.

All ideas of God, indeed, like all religious beliefs, are religious symbols. This is as true of the subtle and intellectualized
conceptions of the philosophers as of the simple, concrete and
familiar images the unreflective man borrows from his experience
with his fellows. It is not that the philosopher is right while the
average man is wrong, that the former's conceptions are true
while the latter's are false. It is not even that the thinker's ideas
are more adequate than the images of the practical man. The
two sets of concepts of God we have been distinguishing both
perform necessary and fundamental religious functions. But the
two functions are so different that they do not compete. The
concrete images of religious practice are in nowise discredited
by the refined concepts of the philosophical theologian. In the
religious life they are indeed more fundamental. For without
them men could hardly worship or pray at all, while the great

majority could and do easily dispense with the concepts which reflective men find necessary in the interests of intellectual consistency. Only for intellectuals are intellectual symbols a religious necessity.

But different as their functions are, both sets of ideas serve as religious symbols. What this means negatively is clear: neither set is literally true, neither is correct, neither gives exact knowledge. To think that either set of ideas does function to produce knowledge and literal truth leads to muddles, mistakes and confusions. Above all, it generates that intolerance which leads men to judge that all ideas of God save their own are false and blasphemous, and to insist that to be saved all men must subscribe to creeds embodying their own prejudices and partial insights.

But what religious symbols do not do is after all not so important as the functions they do perform. This latter is a complex matter difficult to formulate and state satisfactorily. In answering our questions as to the role of knowledge and truth in the religious life, it is necessary to dwell for a little on the positive functions of religious symbols, and on the way in which even those symbols whose primary role is clearly noncognitive nevertheless do contribute to what has always been described as a "revelation" of truth. In this attempt to elucidate a very complicated matter, I shall state some of the conclusions to which I have been led, if not always he, as a result of various seminars I have been privileged to conduct jointly with Paul Tillich.

At the outset it is necessary to draw a sharp distinction between a symbol and a sign. A sign is something which provokes the same human response as some other thing, for which it can hence stand as a kind of surrogate or substitute. A sign hence stands for or represents something other than itself: it is always a sign *of* something else. In contrast, a symbol is in no sense representative: it does not stand for or take the place of anything other than itself. Rather, it *does* something in its own right: it provokes a characteristic response in men. The terminology is not yet settled on this point; but the distinction is fundamental, though the particular way of expressing it is in the present state of usage arbitrary. It is important to realize that religious symbols are not signs; they belong rather with the nonrepresentative symbols which function in various ways in both intellectual and practical life.

A further distinction is also necessary. Some symbols, without being themselves directly representative, or standing for any other identifiable thing, except, perhaps, for certain intellectual processes, nevertheless play an important part in activities that are cognitive, that is, which eventuate in knowledge and truth. The body of scientific concepts, hypotheses, and theories is full of such nonrepresentative but *cognitive* symbols. An instance is the notion of "velocity at an instant." In contrast, there are other symbols, like those that play a role in social processes and in art, whose function is not to participate in activities that eventuate in knowledge, but to lead to other kinds of consequences. What is important to recognize is that religious symbols belong with social and artistic symbols, in the group of symbols that are both *nonrepresentative* and *noncognitive*. Such noncognitive symbols can be said to symbolize not some external thing that can be indicated apart from their operation, but rather what they themselves *do,* their peculiar functions.

Just what is it that such noncognitive symbols do? In the first place, all of them, including religious symbols, provoke in men an emotional response, and stimulate appropriate human activities. In traditional terms, they act on the will rather than on the intellect. They act as motives, they lead to action on the part of the men who are influenced by them. They do not, like signs, merely lead the mind to other things; they produce results in conduct.

Secondly, they provoke in a group of men, the community for whom they serve as symbols, a common or shared response.

They stimulate joint or cooperative activity. This response can become individualized; but even then its individual form is derivative from what is fundamentally a social or group response. The response is common or shared, although the "meaning" of the symbol, that is, its relations to other elements of men's experience, would receive a different intellectual interpretation from different members of the group or symbol community. Thus a physical social symbol, like the flag, or an intellectual social symbol, like the "state" or "liberty," would be fitted in quite differently with other ideas by different men, though all would be stimulated to patriotic emotions and activities, or to libertarian feelings and attitudes.

Thirdly, noncognitive symbols are able to communicate qualitative or "shared" experience, experience that is difficult to put into precise words or statements, and may well be ineffable. This is particularly clear with artistic symbols: they act powerfully in men's experience, but it is notoriously almost impossible to state exactly what they "mean." Needless to say, such artistic symbols must be carefully distinguished from what are often indeed called "symbols" in works of art, but what are really representative signs—signs of something else. It is just that element in a poetic metaphor that is lost through translation into common prose that distinguishes the symbol that is at work from the element of mere sign.

Religious symbols share with other noncognitive symbols these three characteristics. But in addition, and fourthly, religious symbols in particular can be said to "disclose" or "reveal" something about the world in which they function. It is at just this point that we come to the relation between religious symbols and what is usually called religious "knowledge," which is peculiarly close with those intellectual religious symbols that are religious beliefs or ideas. It is this, for instance, that led Goodenough to say, in the passage quoted in the previous chapter, that "there is a large measure of truth in many of our projections." What is it about religious symbols that drives men who have just rejected the notion that religious beliefs are literally true to go on to say things like this?

Religious symbols are commonly said to "reveal" some "truth" about experience. If we ask what it is that such symbols do reveal or disclose about the world, it is clear that it is not what we should call in the ordinary sense "knowledge," in the sense already defined. This revelation can be styled "knowledge" or "truth" only in a sense that is "equivocal" or metaphorical. It is more like direct acquaintance than descriptive knowledge: it resembles what we call "insight" or "vision." Such symbols do not "tell" us anything that is verifiably so; they rather make us "see" something about our experience and our experienced world.

What such a symbol does disclose can be best approached by asking how it is that we gain "insight" into the character and nature of another human personality. By external observation of his behavior, by watching him act and listening to him talk, we can learn much "knowledge" about him that is clearly gained by methods not essentially different from those by which we gain "knowledge" about the behavior of other things in our natural world. But intimate acquaintance with another human personality acquired through a long experience of friendship or of love, can give us an "insight" into the essence of the man that cannot be won by any merely external observation of his behavior. When certain of his acts or words "reveal" to us what he "really is," as we put it, we often say that they are "symbols" of his true character and nature. The gifted biographer or historian often has such "insight" into the persons he is trying to grasp. Ernst Cassirer had a genius for this kind of insight, and he erected a whole theory of historical knowledge around this process of what he called "symbolic interpretation." What Wilhelm Dilthey called *Verstehen* has been grossly abused by many German sociologists, but it has a genuine application if anywhere to the knowledge of human personality.

Just what does this process of symbolic interpretation mean? It seems, first, that such symbolic acts or words concentrate and sum up and unify a long and intimate experience we have enjoyed of a person, or a long and close study we have made of a figure's activities. Secondly, they reveal possibilities and powers latent in his nature. For what a man "really is" is not exhausted in what he has already done, in his past behavior that is on the record. It is what he *can* do, the powers he has in him. All knowledge of anything is ultimately a knowledge of its powers and possibilities. But clearly the distinction between what any being has done and what that being can do, is most striking and significant in the case of human personality.

The example of human personality has always seemed the best clue to the way of conceiving the Divine in the world, even when men have gone on to recognize that the religious dimension of existence ultimately transcends personality. Generalizing the function of symbols in coming to know persons, we may say that a religious symbol unifies and sums up and brings to a focus men's long and intimate experience of their universe and of what it offers to human life. As John Dewey says of the work of art in general, it "operates imaginatively rather than in the realm of physical existences. What it does is to concentrate and enlarge an immediate experience." [3]

In so doing, religious symbols seem to disclose or reveal powers and possibilities inherent in the nature of things. They serve, that is, not as instruments of a "knowledge" based on an experience of what the world has done, of how it has behaved and acted in the past, of the resources it has been found to provide for men, but rather as instruments of "insight" and "vision," of what it could do, of what it might offer, of what it might become and be. Religious symbols are thus like Platonic Ideas, which themselves developed from a refinement of the Pythagorean religious symbols: they do not tell us that anything is so, they rather make us see something. They enable us to discern possi-

[3] John Dewey, *Art as Experience,* p. 273.

bilities beyond the actual, powers not yet fully realized; and in so doing they disclose what the nature of things "really is." Like Platonic Ideas, religious symbols are closely connected with the power of intellectual vision, *Nous,* the power of "imagination," if the imagination be the organ of intellectual vision.

And so religious symbols, through concentrating the long experience of a people, and the insights of its prophets and saints, seem to serve as instruments of revelation, of vision— of a vision of the powers and possibilities in the world. They disclose what Paul Tillich calls, in symbolic terms, "the power of Being." They lead to a vision of man in the world, of the human situation in its cosmic setting, and to use Tillich's term again, of man's "ultimate concern." Speaking most generally, they lead to a vision of the Divine, what the Christian symbol has called the *visio Dei* and the *fruitio Dei.* They serve the chief end of man, "to glorify God and enjoy Him forever." It is impossible even to state this function of religious symbols except in symbolic terms. For it is clear that all formulations of these visions, all ways of imagining and conceiving the Divine, all ideas of God, whether those employed in the practice of the religious arts, like worship or prayer, or the refined and subtle concepts of the great philosophical theologians, are religious symbols. Only through symbols can we approach the Divine, only thus can we indicate the religious dimension of life in the world. We cannot see God face to face. This latter is itself a symbolic statement.

Let us then try to express the power of religious vision in another symbolic language. It is man who discerns Perfection shining through the world's imperfections in a dimly reflected splendor. Yet this experience of the Divine splendors suggested in the world, of human life variously illuminated as by a light that is eternal, has seemed to point to a source of that light. In locating this source of splendor, Christianity has alternated over the centuries between expressing a temper of humanism and a temper of humility. At certain periods it has emphasized the humanistic faith of the Greek Fathers, that the source is to be sought in the rationality and moral power of man himself, naturally inhering in him and sustained by the universe about him. At other times it has shared the Augustinian distrust of man, and felt that it is to be sought beyond man and nature, illuminating them and sustaining them from without, wholly beyond man's control, breaking through and grasping him in ecstatic experience.

Our own science and philosophy likewise point in both these two directions. For them also man catches the gleam of an eternal perfection. But "Divinity" they have come to construe as a quality to be discriminated in human experience of the world, the splendor of the vision that sees beyond the actual into the perfected and eternal realm of the imagination. Such a world is human experience purified and recast in the crucible of imaginative vision, an experience that has laid off the garments of time to partake of eternity. Yet for us too this timeless vision is of something inescapably real. And it is no mere dream created by the spirit of man. It is nature herself coming to a fuller realization of her suggested possibilities in the imagination of man.

There is much that suggests that today the twin qualities of power and perfection, the two aspects of the Divine traditionally symbolized as God, have come to impinge upon us from different quarters, and not as from a single ray of light. There are many for whom religion has become a devotion to the ideal, a devotion inspired by a sense of the worth of human personality as its source. They feel intensely the splendor shining through man, so intensely that what is not revealed in the highest human qualities there suggested—mere cosmic power or intelligibility, for instance—cannot for them possess the supreme value of the Divine. Much of our liberal religion, in fact if not yet in symbol, has become such a merely human and social idealism. There are others for whom such purely human values are all too petty and ignoble, to whom salvation comes rather from elevating the spirit to cosmic impartiality, to the majesty and order of the universe. For such, religion is a cosmic sense, a recognition of man's utter dependence on a power which yet satisfies the demand of his intellect for understanding. And for the Spinozas and the Einsteins such a religion does afford a peace intense if austere. There too strikes the splendor of the Divine.

Does the light then fall only on nature, the impartial author of good and evil? Is it through the natural order that the splendor shines most brightly? But it is man alone who realizes, if imperfectly, her highest possibilities, who discerns the cosmic order and beauty. Does it fall only on the ideal which man beholds in vision? Does not the beholder shine even more gloriously than that which is beheld? For the vision fades and passes, but the human spirit advances to fresh vision. Is it then man himself who is the source, man the creature of nature who alone of all her products perfects what she has left imperfect? But is it not nature who reveals her possibilities to man and affords him the power which sustains his vision? Where, indeed, is the Divine to be discerned?

The question remains whether one single symbol can still serve us for the natural order, for its manifestations in the human spirit, and for its perfecting in the vision of that spirit. Our experience seems to have grown more plural: we now respect and use nature, while we consecrate ourselves to its possibilities as transformed in the spirit of man. Our experience of Divinity, in truth, seems manifold: it is only to faith that the Divine is one. The splendor falls on nature, on man, and on that which nature provokes man to discern. But to us it seems a different splendor, and it is on the human spirit in vision calling forth in its fellows answering vision that it seems to fall most gloriously.

In many and diverse places, and through the lens of many and diverse symbols, man has discerned the Divine splendor. To push this symbolic language further, we might speak of the Divine as the "order of splendor," found in our experience of the world, that revealing light which falls so variously upon our life. If the highest it permits us to discern be not the idealized possibilities of nature and of associated human living, but that very gift of vision it brings to the spirit of man, then, still speaking symbolically, God may well be for us the total order of that which has the power to evoke such vision. The Divine awakens our insight in the majesty and system of the universe; it awakens it more directly in the aspiration of our fellow men, dimly striving for contact with the eternal. It awakens it most of all in the vision of a fellow spirit kindling our own vision. And Christianity has found its own most distinctive symbol in the living God revealed to men through incarnation in the vision of Jesus.

It might be better to say, a symbol is functioning religiously, and the vision it makes us see is genuinely religious, only if the symbol does reveal man's ultimate concern, does disclose the Divine. In the last chapter we tried to delimit in a preliminary way what is the distinctive thing that religion and religious symbols do in human life, what is involved in "functioning religiously." We have now come somewhat closer to a statement, not of all the many things religion does for man, but of what the essential religious function is. On the one hand, religion is a practical commitment to certain values. Religious symbols serve to strengthen that kind of religious commitment; to strengthen men's "faith," to intensify and enhance and clarify a practical commitment to one's "ultimate concern." On the other hand, religion is the vision of the Divine; the awareness of the religious dimension of experience and of the world, the awareness of the "order of splendor," and the fostering and clarification of that awareness.

Practical commitment and vision are of course in no sense to be divided or divorced from each other. But men are in the end saved, I am convinced, by vision rather than by works. I find I am not descended from a long line of Calvinists in vain. To be sure, works are the only test of vision, and for most men the vision seems to come only through works and in the midst of works. Our busy and activistic American approach to life leads most of us to emphasize the works, the practical commitment, the function of religious symbols and beliefs in strengthening religious faith. But my own temper and experience have led me to take the vision of God as more inclusive as well as more ultimate than the practical commitment. For the vision does seem to issue necessarily in a commitment, while the practical commitment often fails to include much of vision. "This is life eternal, that they should know thee the only true God."

But religious symbols not only reveal the powers and possibilities latent in the nature of things. These powers and possibilities are encountered as very complex. In the vision they become unified; in a genuine sense the disclosure is the revelation of their unification. To faith the Divine is one. Hence religious symbols serve not only as instruments of *revelation,* they are at the same time instruments of *unification.* They unify men's experience in terms of what might well be called their "organizing concern"; they unify the world in the light of men's vision of the Divine. To reveal and unify the powers and possibilities inherent in the religious dimension that man's experience of the world discloses, in the "order of splendor," seems to be a way of stating the distinctive function of religious symbols.

We have made it clear that the insight and vision revealed by even intellectual religious symbols, by religious beliefs, can scarcely be called "knowledge" or "truth," except in a Pickwickian and equivocal sense. Yet there still seems to remain something unsatisfactory about the complete denial of all cognitive values to religious beliefs. We do speak about "religious knowledge," and about the "truths" of faith. We speak likewise about the "truth" of the revelations of art, and about an "artistic knowledge" which is denied to the methods of scientific inquiry. Such artistic "knowledge," we are careful to add if we are wise, is very unlike the knowledge that can be expressed in exact statements. And artistic "truth" is so different from the truths that are the product of our elaborate processes of verification that most students of the theory of knowledge today would hold that little but confusion and obliteration of necessary and vital distinctions is generated by calling two such diverse things by the same term. Indeed, there is a philosophic view widespread in our time that "truth" should be restricted to the products of scientific inquiry in a rather narrow sense, so that it is inappropriate, or even "meaningless," to speak even of "moral truth."

Such views, of course, immediately provoke the rejoinder: there must then be many other kinds of "truth" than the scientist's: moral, artistic, religious, and the rest. And this notion that there is a "knowledge" and a "truth" different in kind from that of science, whether of art or of religion, is historically a heritage from the Romantic philosophies that were protesting against just such a rigid, unimaginative, and sterile adherence to a narrow scientific ideal. But after all, this "extranaturalism" or transcendentalism was the great support and the fundamental conviction of all the Romantic philosophies of protest against the limitations of eighteenth-century rationalism. Was there really no significant insight in this protest? Specifically, can the artist, the prophet and the saint show us something that can not inappropriately be called "truth"? Is there any religious "knowledge" significantly different from the verifiable and explanatory knowledge of scientific truths, so that the two never compete but rather supplement each other?

With proper and careful qualification, it seems that the facts do suggest to a sensitive and candid mind that the answer is, yes, there is. That is why, in stating at the outset the three major positions on the place of knowledge and truth in the religious life, it was pointed out that there seem to be essential values in this (then listed as the second position) that could not be lightly abandoned. Just what, then, may be the character of this religious "knowledge" that needs to be carefully set off from knowledge as it is ordinarily understood and as it has so far been here defined—from the explanatory and verifiable truths of common sense and of scientific inquiry?

In trying to answer this question, we can find help by examining the enterprise of art. Indeed, I have discovered that whenever in my thinking I take religion as one art among many others, and begin to consider it in the terms appropriate to the other arts or *technai,* things at once begin to happen for me intellectually.[4] I am led on to fruitful and suggestive analogies that illuminate the religious life for me as no other approach seems to do. I should hold, in fact, that all the major human enterprises, those that Santayana admits to "ideal society," and that Hegel held to belong to *Absoluter Geist,* are most fruitfully to be considered as arts, including the art of inquiry, or science; and are most revealingly treated in terms of the concepts that make an art intelligible. I have long found most suggestive the view expressed by John Dewey in the ninth chapter of his *Experience and Nature,* "Experience, Nature and Art," that "art" or technē is the most inclusive metaphysical category. This view

[4] Paul Tillich speaks for the religious tradition, though his accents are as usual his own, in commenting on this taking of religion as an "art": "Your use of the term 'art' for religion is meaningful in the context in which you use it, namely, as a human function. But religion itself claims that as a human function it is only the receiving part of a divine act of revelatory character. I myself interpret it as an ecstatic experience of being grasped. Can this be combined with your terminology?"

It is doubtful whether "religion itself" makes any claims at all, though there is no doubt about the claims of the Lutheran tradition. But Mr. Tillich's question seems to spring from a misconceiving of the way in which I would construe any "art." An art is not merely a "human function"; it is not just an activity that belongs exclusively to man. It is something man does, but he does it because something in the world provokes him to do it; and what he does is carried on in cooperation with the world, its materials, its activities, its possibilities. An art is thus genuinely a joint activity in which man and certain portions and aspects of the world work together.

Hence the art of religion includes both the human function and the "divine action." To conceive religion in terms of the human function alone is to adopt the position that is usually called today "religious humanism." Such a narrowly conceived "humanism" is an impossible interpretation of the art of religion, or indeed of any other art, for our present-day naturalistic philosophizing. And it would certainly present a sharply truncated version of the facts of the religious life.

For the character of the action of the religious dimension of the world upon us, see the treatment of "revelation" on page 130. Whether the terminology there adopted is successfully combined with Mr. Tillich's is for the Teutonic Ground of Being alone to decide.

is set forth in very similar terms, incidentally, by the early Schelling of the *Identitätsphilosophie.*[5]

What Dewey himself says about the relation between art and knowledge has a most distinct relevance to the art of religion in particular. "The sense of increase of understanding, of a deepened intelligibility on the part of objects of nature and man, resulting from esthetic experience, has led philosophic theorists to treat art as a mode of knowledge, and has induced artists, especially poets, to regard art as a mode of revelation of the inner nature of things that cannot be had in any other way. It has led to treating art as a mode of knowledge superior not only to that of ordinary life but to that of science itself. . . . The assertion has been expressly made by many philosophers. . . . The varieties of incompatible conceptions put forth prove that the philosophers in question were anxious to carry a dialectical development of conceptions framed without regard to art into esthetic experience more than they were willing to allow this experience to speak for itself." [6] This is obviously true in the art of religion: "religious experience" has again and again been made to illustrate and confirm some prevailing philosophical or scientific theory.

"Nevertheless, the sense of disclosure and heightened intelligibility of the world remains to be accounted for. . . . I cannot find in [the remarks of Wordsworth, Shelley, and other Romantic poets] any intention to assert that esthetic experience is to be *defined* as a mode of knowledge. What is intimated to my mind, is, that in both production and enjoyed perception of works of art, knowledge is transformed; it becomes something more than knowledge because it is merged with non-intellectual elements to form an experience worth while as an experience. . . .

"Tangled scenes of life are made more intelligible in esthetic

[5] See Schelling's *System des transcendentalischen Idealismus,* Einleitung, Sec. 3; Sechster Hauptabschnitt.

[6] John Dewey, *Art as Experience,* pp. 288-289.

experience: not, however, as reflection and science render things more intelligible by reduction to conceptual form, but by presenting their meanings as the matter of a clarified, coherent, and intensified or 'impassioned' experience." The phrase Dewey uses for what art does with knowledge is peculiarly applicable to what the religious arts do with the secular knowledge they take over and consecrate: "The transformation of knowledge that is effected in emotional and imaginative vision." [7]

What Dewey says about this imaginative vision in all the arts seems to apply with particular force to the art of religion: "Imaginative vision is the power that unifies all the constituents of the matter of a work of art, making a whole out of them in all their variety. Yet all the elements of our being that are displayed in special emphases and partial realizations in other experiences are merged in esthetic experience. And they are so completely merged in the immediate wholeness of the experience that each is submerged:—it does not present itself in consciousness as a distinct element." [8]

I must confess that my own intellectual experience with the thought of John Dewey has invariably been that, after painfully working out what seemed to me a fairly adequate solution of a philosophic problem, I have then turned to his writings, only to discover that he had already stated my conclusions far better than I had been able to do. But his way of arriving at what is obviously the philosophic truth, since we always seem to agree in the end, has never been mine. And strive as I might, I have never been able to write in the language of John Dewey. In fact, I have not often striven. For these compelling reasons, what I want to say about what the analogy of the other arts suggests to my mind about the art of religion, in this matter of religious "knowledge," will have to make a fresh start.

The aesthetically sensitive painter or poet can notice further features in the seeing of grass, for example, than the mere "green"

[7] *Ibid.,* pp. 289-290.
[8] *Ibid.,* p. 274.

that suffices for most practical purposes. He brings to the visual transaction an experience, a skill, a trained art of perceiving, that enables him to qualify that transaction in new ways; and he can communicate these newly revealed qualities in his particular language or medium. He can thus reveal unsuspected powers and possibilities of being seen, resident in the visible world—unsuspected qualities in grass, to take our example. Chinese and Japanese painters are notoriously good at this; so, in very different fashion, are the impressionists, and Van Gogh.

This is the source of the enormous fertility of painting or of poetry in revealing new visual, new perceptual powers in things—in "enhancing the significance," as we say, of the visible world—in disclosing "new meanings and consummatory experiences," as Dewey puts it. The painter can qualify, not merely his canvas, and not merely our experience, but also the visible world itself with new qualities hitherto unsuspected. The artist through his products *does* certain things to us, he affects certain changes in us and in our world. He "reconstructs our experience," says our theory: the work of art is to educate and re-educate us. In other words, the artist seems to be teaching us something, about the world and about ourselves, about ourselves in our world. That is why we are tempted, despite all the difficulties and paradoxes to which that leads, to say that he is increasing our "knowledge" and teaching us "truth"—"artistic truth," we sometimes call it. Painting, poetry, music, religion, all the arts, do indeed "teach" us something. They may not teach us *that* anything is so. We have seen the reasons why it seems inappropriate to say that the various arts teach us propositional knowledge. They do not "explain" the world in the sense of accounting for it; rather they "explain" it in the sense of making plain its features. But they certainly teach us *how to do* something better. The painter shows us how to see the visible world better, the world of color and form—how to see grass better.

Just what does the artist teach? The painter clearly teaches us how to see selected aspects of the world more adequately than we could without his assistance. Sometimes he teaches us how to see the face of nature or of the works of man; sometimes he teaches us how to see another human being. At bottom he teaches us how to see color, form, their relations and qualities. He reveals possibilities and powers we had not noticed. He enables us to see what can be done with lines, masses, colors, with the features of nature, with the gestures and attitudes of men, with the symbols in terms of which men lead their emotional lives. The composer teaches us how to hear sounds better, how they can be put together, how they can illustrate a pattern of musical logic and dialectic, how they can create a world of pure and unalloyed form. He teaches us how emotion can be expressed, communicated, and resolved through a purge of pity and terror. The poet teaches us the music and the logic of words and language, the feel of words and the feeling of life as lived. He teaches us the emotional intensity of thought.

The work of the painter, the musician, the poet, teaches us how to use our eyes, our ears, our minds, and our feelings with greater power and skill. It teaches us how to become more aware both of what is and of what might be, in the world that offers itself to our sensitive receptivity. It shows us how to discern unsuspected qualities in the world encountered, latent powers and possibilities there resident. Still more, it makes us see the new qualities with which that world, in cooperation with the spirit of man, can clothe itself. For art is an enterprise in which the world and man are most genuinely cooperative, and in which the working together of natural materials and powers and of human techniques and vision is most clearly creative of new qualities and powers.

Is it otherwise with the prophet and the saint? They too can do something to us, they too can effect changes in us and in our world. They too can teach us something, about our world and about ourselves. They teach us how to see what man's life in the world is, and what it might be. They teach us how to discern what human nature can make out of its natural conditions and materials. They reveal latent powers and possibilities not previously noticed. They make us receptive to qualities of the world encountered; and they open our hearts to the new qualities with which that world, in cooperation with the spirit of man, can clothe itself. They enable us to see and feel the religious dimension of our world better, the "order of splendor," and of man's experience in and with it. They teach us how to find the Divine; they show us visions of God.

Is all this properly to be called "knowledge," all that the painter, the composer, the poet, that the prophet and the saint can teach us? It is clearly not "knowledge" as we have so far defined it. It is not the kind of knowledge that can be put into words and statements, and set down in manuals of aesthetics or theology. It cannot be formulated in neat handbooks of "How to Look at the Visible World," or "How to See the Divine." It is not the aesthetician with his analyses, the critic with his rules, the theologian with his propositions, who teaches us these things. It is rather the painter with his painting, the musician with his thematic development, the poet with his sonnet, the prophet with his vision of righteousness, the saint with his quality of holiness, who teaches us how to discern better, who reveals the new qualities and possibilities of the world. The knowledge so taught is not an explanation or account of anything. It is not something that can be formulated as a set of rationally demonstrated conclusions. It cannot even be warranted by any precise method of experimental confirmation, though it clearly has its own standards of adequacy. It is more like an art, a technique, of how to see and discern and feel more fully, of how to use the materials of experience to create what was not before.

But surely we Americans, with our devotion to technical intelligence, would be willing to call this ability "knowledge." "Artistic knowledge," or "religious knowledge," if we are to use the terms at all, it is suggested, must be taken, not as the truth of the propositions of science, but as what we Americans have come to call a "know-how." It is *knowing how* to qualify the world with those qualities appropriate to each art, knowing how to be receptive toward them, and how to make them a part of our experience and of our lives. A "know-how," however, though it may well be said to be "cognitive," does not seem to be appropriately judged as either "true" or "false." That is why it seems preferable to speak of this "know-how" of religion as religious "knowledge" rather than as religious "truth." Its standards are clearly different from those of propositions.[9]

Moreover, such processes of qualification, receiving, and assimilating are, I take it, just what we mean by "revealing" or "disclosing." For the qualities that are the outcome of these processes, qualities that impose themselves upon us and are received, are in a genuine sense qualities of the world. It is not we men who in our wisdom create them. What the painter, the poet, or the prophet has done can be accurately said to be to "reveal" or "disclose" to us authentic powers in things. Just as in the visual situation the grass is qualified by "green," has become "green," and really *is* green, so in the aesthetic situation it has become qualified by aesthetic qualities, and *is* beautiful.

[9] In the second chapter of his *Concept of Mind* (1949), "Knowing How and Knowing That," Gilbert Ryle makes the same distinction between propositional knowledge and "know-how." He is contrasting "intellectual" operations with "intelligent" practice, and arguing against the "intellectualist legend" that intelligence or know-how always involves putting into practice certain prior propositions. He concludes: "Efficient practice precedes the theory of it. . . . 'Intelligent' cannot be defined in terms of 'intellectual' or 'knowing *how*' in terms of 'knowing *that*.' We learn *how* by practice, schooled indeed by criticism and example, but often quite unaided by any lessons in theory." (pp. 30, 32, 41.)

"Knowing how" Ryle takes as a complex dispositional property. Our knowledge of the "know-how" possessed by someone else he takes to be a knowledge of powers and possibilities—the kind of "knowledge" we have found religious symbols revealing. "True, we go beyond what we see them do and hear them say, but this going beyond is not a going behind, in the sense of making inference to occult causes; it is going beyond, in the sense of considering, in the first instance, the powers and propensities of which their actions are exercises." (p. 51.)

Ryle does not himself apply these distinctions to religious knowledge. Like Dewey, Ryle is a thinker at whose conclusions I often find I have myself arrived by a different path.

Just so, in the religious situation, in religious experience, the world is qualified by "the Divine," has become "Divine," and really *is* Divine. In each case what is revealed is the power of actualizing such a qualification, the world's power of acting upon us, and our power of knowing how to welcome that action— a joint power both of seeing and of being seen, of discerning and of revealing.[10]

Again, as a discoverer of new powers and possibilities the painter has much in common with the scientist. What he does with and makes out of what forces itself upon his attention and what he sees, by selecting from it, manipulating it, reorganizing and reconstructing it by means of his distinctive art, is very much like what the experimentation of the scientist effects. Both the scientist and the artist, by revealing new powers, and by pushing back the limits set to the operation of things, enlarge our horizons, increase our knowledge, and extend our powers. This suggests that, to perform his function successfully, the artist, like the scientist, should be accorded by right the freest possible experimentation with and manipulation of his materials, and that he should likewise recognize the obligation to bring to his

[10] It has been attempted here to state both sides of the religious transaction: the action of the Divine in revealing itself to men, and the human discerning and receiving of that revelation. Religious "knowledge" is knowing how to discern and receive what is revealed. The "self-revelation of the Divine" is what Mr. Tillich, in his comment in note 4 on page 124, calls "a divine act of revelatory character." The "human discerning and receiving" is what he calls "the receiving part" of the religious transaction. There is clearly activity on both sides, and both activities are involved in the transaction. Which of the two shall be emphasized constitutes one of the cardinal differences in men's religious experience. To lay stress on the human discerning of the Divine is to express the religious temper of humanism; to place it on the self-revealing is to express the temper of humility. Mr. Tillich's "ecstatic experience of being grasped" by the Divine is an excellent religious symbol for the latter. My own experience has led me to attempt at least to put an equal emphasis on both of the two activities involved in the religious transaction. Both seem to be necessary and essential for religion.

Every art seems to display the same cooperation between the activities of man and of his world. The side of "being grasped" has been made central in art at least since Plato's *Io*.

manipulation the widest possible past experience and store of resources. Both are essential to the artistic transaction. And dare I add that the activities of the prophet and the saint also resemble the experimentation of the scientist and are subject to the same controlling conditions? We need as many varying visions of God as we can possibly share. Many radically different visions have been beheld, and so long as the world has man in it, many more will be. Every new prophet's vision, like every new poem, will reveal new possibilities in the world. Visions are many, and many are the unified visions to which they can be pushed; but there is no unity of the visions of God. In that sense, the revelation of the Divine is not and can never be completed.[11]

In any event, if we feel justified in speaking of religious "knowledge" at all, this must be carefully and precisely distinguished from the scientific knowledge of descriptive and explanatory statement. The traditional Augustinian distinction is between *scientia* and *sapientia,* between "science" and "wisdom." Paul Tillich, wisely preferring that most philosophic of languages, the Greek, makes the essential distinction between *episteme* and *gnosis.* With his emphasis on religious "knowledge" as what he calls "participating knowledge," he is even willing to compare *gnosis* or religious "knowledge" with what Holy Writ points to when it states that Abraham went in unto Sarah and "knew" her.

The suggestion here is to use the American tongue, and to distinguish between "science," and "technology" or "invention"—between science and "know-how." Religious "knowledge" is not mystic intuition, it is not the awareness of values, it is not the encounter with "the Holy," it is not existential commitment to the will to believe. It is rather a technical skill, an art, a "know-

---

[11] It is this fundamental and overwhelming fact that has led to the view that the Divine itself—the religious dimension of the world, as we have been inadequately calling it—is not completed, but is growing and developing and taking on ever deeper forms. Such a symbol indeed expresses much profound human experience in the Romantic and evolutionary eras; and the history of religious "revelation" or "insight" would offer much to bear it out.

how." Within a broad "knowledge" we shall then distinguish between propositional knowledge, which must be either true or false, and "know-how," which is neither true nor false, but adequate and effective for its purposes or not. And thus the revelation which is the distinctive function of religious symbols, including religious beliefs, turns out in the last analysis to be the disclosing of a "know-how," a revelation of how to become aware of the world's religious dimension, of how to see God and enjoy him forever.

Significantly, also, all these various teachers—painter, poet, musician, prophet, and saint—"know how" to unify their vision. And they can teach us how to unify our own experience. In his artistic product the artist unifies the possibilities he discerns in his materials—in his work of art. And the "work" of that work of art unifies the beholder's experience in turn. The prophet and the saint likewise "know how" to unify their vision of the world's possibilities, and they can teach us how to see the vision that will unify the world for us. Religion gives us a "know-how": how to unify our experience through a unified vision of the Divine, of the religious dimension of the world, of the order of splendor. The distinctive character of religious knowledge, which removes it from any competition with other forms of knowing, is that it is, not a unique experience, not a mystic intuition or "knowledge" of some higher realm, but rather an art, a technique, a "know-how"—for opening one's heart to seeing the Divine, for knowing God, in the midst of the conditions of human life in the natural world.

Does this commit us to a religious "truth"? I think and hope not. It seems more confusing than clarifying to speak in such a way. The best name for the test of religious know-how seems to be "adequacy." It is well to keep "truth" for the knowledge that is science, with all its complex procedures and criteria for verifying propositions that can be stated in words. But perhaps the scientists themselves are today abandoning "truth" as the name for the test of their knowledge, for some other property like "confirmability" or "warranted assertibility." And in calling the knowledge that is "know-how" something that is to be judged by its "adequacy," I remember the old definition of "truth" as "adaequation of thing and understanding." Perhaps, after all, we have at last come the full circle. Perhaps it is now the visions of the unified possibilities of the world— of the Divine, of the "order of splendor"—that we are once more permitted to call "true." If so, this "truth" of "know-how" is not to be confused with the warranted knowledge that is science. It is rather that Truth of which it was said of old, "But of all things Truth beareth away the victory," [12] and again, "Ye shall know the Truth, and the Truth shall make you free."

[12] This is the motto inscribed above the door of the School of Theology at Oberlin.

Epilogue. *Apologia pro Theologia Rationali*

If, as we saw in our third chapter, the primary contribution of science to religion today is a scientific understanding of the nature and function of religion itself; and if the conclusion of wide and extensive investigation is that religion is not primarily a way of understanding and explaining, but a way of celebrating, consecrating, and clarifying, what place, then, if any, is to be found in the religious life so understood for knowing, for thinking, for intelligence?

It is clear there is a very subordinate role for scientific doctrines or conclusions. There is in fact but a minor place for them in scientific activities themselves. Scientific theory is exceedingly transitory, and at bottom is essentially mythology or "projection"—a complex set of symbols useful in organizing experimental findings and in forwarding techniques of investigation, a form of "policy-making," as James B. Conant has put it. Consider the theories and doctrines in physics today. Can they be said to be literally "true"? Especially where they touch on beliefs of traditional religious significance: the origin and end of the universe, the nature of its controlling forces, the nature and destiny of man? Physics offers useful but very hypothetical and speculative guesses, to be reconstructed into more adequate ones tomorrow. Psychology, in its turn, suggests Romantic myths, more or less appropriate to the techniques of therapeutic manipulation, themselves of rather dubious validity.

Of course, if we really desire to do so, it is not very difficult to reconcile such current scientific doctrines with *any* religious beliefs. By this late date the wit of man has turned the trick again and again. Theologians have today pretty much abandoned that enterprise of harmonizing science and religion. Perhaps, in the face of our rapidly shifting scientific theories, they have found the task too bewildering. Perhaps they have just tired of it, and set it aside until scientific conclusions achieve more stability. Perhaps they have acquired more sense, and a better appreciation of the religious function of theology, of beliefs. Some of our more recent physicists have indeed rushed in where the angelic doctors have feared to tread, with new and often blasphemous essays in speculative theology. But the reconciling power of the human mind knows no limits. It is obvious that, given time, it can adjust the religious life to any intellectual interpretation of experience, to any "scientific world-view." It can either draw the line carefully between the fields of religion and of science, between the "truths of faith" and the "truths of reason," like Maimonides, Thomas, Kant, or Eddington. Or it can reconstruct both religious beliefs and scientific doctrines in terms of a new and more comprehensive scheme of understanding, like Spinoza, Hegel, Whitehead, or Heidegger. Such reconciliation is especially easy to effect today. For the speculative dogmas of nineteenth-century science that seemed to be opposed to the demands of human personality have either crumbled or are now seen as at best the postulates of scientific inquiry.

In some such fashion, since the time of Philo and the Fourth Gospel, the religious activity of the Western tradition has normally expressed and consecrated intellectual and scientific values. Again and again it has succeeded in effecting a convergence between ultimate religious and scientific ideas. The God of the subtle and the learned has been conceived, as we have seen, as the Logos, the Prime Mover, the Order of Nature, the Newtonian First Force, the Absolute, Evolution, Being. There is little doubt that this intellectual task can be accomplished once more for the distinctive first principles of our own scientific age, and that religious thought, if it really so desire, can reinterpret Hebrew myth and Platonic symbol in terms of the myths and symbols of the science and philosophy of the moment—of its ultimate organizing hypotheses and principles. This is especially likely if our science fulfills its promise of becoming a genuinely social science, and ceases to be merely the abstractions of physics or of psychology, and if our philosophy develops a comprehensive understanding of human life in its natural setting.

This is certainly not the most important religious problem today. It is not even the most important intellectual problem in religion. But it does answer to a human desire and need deeply embedded in our scientific culture. And there is more of value in it than the theological fashions of the moment seem inclined to grant. For better or worse, liberal Protestants and Jews with intellectual interests do want to harmonize religion and science. They do want to employ religious symbols that have a scientific as well as an imaginative and moral relevance and significance. If the figure and image of the God of old will no longer fit today into an accepted and intelligible system of ideas, they want a conception that will. No amount of persuasion, based on a study of religions in general, that theological ideas are techniques in the practice of religion and not explanatory of existence, will convince them that in *their* religion philosophic truth is not an ultimate value. For it so obviously is. Liberal religion has staked its all on humanizing its values and rationalizing its symbols. Its ideals must be adequate to actual human experience, and its beliefs must be compatible with current scientific truth. And there is a profoundly religious reason underlying this irresistible craving. In the interests of religion itself, the religious life must make a central place for intellectual values. In our day and generation we have learned what happens when it does not.

"This is life eternal, that they should know thee the only true God." So runs Holy Writ, in accord with the divine Plato. Not to build a new social order, not to celebrate experience with appropriate techniques, preferably with music by Bach, not to inculcate the power of positive thinking, but to *know* God. Notoriously, no really up-to-date religious thinker any longer "knows God." There are plenty who use him for some good purpose, and plenty who take his name in vain. Contemporary religion, as we have seen, is split among those who follow the prophet who would make all things new, those who follow the priest who would celebrate a complacent existence through the expected forms of ritual, and those who follow the healer who would minister to a mind diseased. We are divided between building the new Jerusalem, pronouncing a decent formula for hallowing a prosperous life, and inspiring confident living or the courage to be. No one, it seems, is so poor as to honor the theologian who seeks to know God. The theologians themselves are vying to insist that theology is not a form of knowledge, but the symbol of something else not intellectual at all: of moral values and social objectives, of aesthetic thrills and yearnings, or of therapeutic techniques. Since the theologians refuse to find any place for intelligibility, the physicists rush in to identify God with the "cosmic yeast." Whether religion be a crusade against the profit system, or a delicious feeling in the spine, or an amateur psychotherapy, or the blasphemies of mathematical physicists tempted by Gifford lectureships, no one today, it is clear, bothers to know God.

Is there then no place at all in our present-day religion for knowing, for thinking, for intelligence? We have seen that all studies of primitive religion make it primarily a way of acting and feeling, of fostering group integration, and only incidentally a way of thinking. In the desire to regain for religion something of its lost power as a social bond, it is doubtless natural to try by subordinating intellectual values to make it as primitive as possible. Students of religion might well view with great approbation the success of our modern American religion in approaching such primitive mindlessness. If human morality and human reason are as nothing in the face of the Eternal Judge, or of the Unconditioned, it is hardly surprising that if religion be taken as a crusade, it should be a crusade with little morality or reason in it. If the Christians in Germany had known God better, and had not come to despise thinking, I wonder whether it would have been quite so easy for "German Christians" to think of Hitler as his incarnation. If we had not insisted so strongly that theology is mythology, and must not try to be literally true, I wonder whether there would have been found such ready acceptance for the "myth of the twentieth century," whose chief claim to our attention was its complete lack of truth. If theology be not science, but a religious technique for expressing deeply felt emotion, if God be not the object toward which the religious life is directed, to be clarified by reflection, but part of its apparatus, to be used by that emotion, there can really be little objection if in Germany—and nearer home—theology and God have been patently used to organize popular hysteria with a perfection of technique.

Can the religious life really afford to turn its back on all knowing and intelligence? For if religion be a celebration and a consecration of the values of life, as the instrument of group integration and cohesion, but not a consecration of moral and intellectual ends, which are left to be sought elsewhere; if the beliefs of religious faith be not "true," but only good, and if truth be exiled to another area of experience; then the life celebrated will surely have little moral or intellectual quality, and its ends will hardly be truly good. If religion does not celebrate intelligence, then the values it does celebrate will lack intellectual clarification and criticism. The celebrants will express moral sentimentality and intellectual confusion, and the morally enlightened and intellectually clearheaded will scarcely enjoy or participate in the celebration. That much in liberal religion in America, and in its alienation of those with moral and intellectual integrity, may be so described today, is notorious. And if the religious instrument of group cohesion is to be a technique for organizing feeling and emotion, but not thought, by a mythology that must not aim at literal truth, then it need scarcely occasion surprise if the group religion is used to organize and express a complacent acquiescence in the worst features of the American ethos. For all this, our half-understood theory gives its blessing: men need not seek to know God.

If we are not all wholly happy with the primitive religion

we seem well on the way to achieving (a headline for the 1955 report of the National Council ran, "Church Bodies Gain Members; Morality Falls Off"); if religion be not merely a celebration but also a clarification of values, then to clarify values surely calls for thinking and intelligence. It is not enough to take the name of the Lord in vain, or to use him for some worthy purpose: we need to *know* something about God. The celebration of the life in which intelligence is to play a part must express and consecrate and clarify intellectual values. It must in some central sense embody truth. That is why those who insist on bringing their religious beliefs into accord with philosophic truth are right. That is why the enterprise of rational theology has a value that is not only intellectual but genuinely religious. Its worth lies not in the formulations of the moment—they will soon give way to others. It lies rather in the conviction that it is supremely important to make the never ending effort to understand. And that is an eternal religious need. For those who feel it it will be devoted to the use of intelligence in all the profounder ways in which it can serve religious faith and vision.

The most important function of intelligence and science in the religious life is to examine intelligently the values it is expressing. We need have little fear, or hope, that if our traditional faith disintegrates, as it has in many parts of Europe, we shall be left without any religious faith at all. Recent experience has ruled out the expectation of any such vacuum. The pressing problem is, rather, what can science and intelligence do with the new religious faiths that will take its place? If we can no longer find our historic religion meaningful, we shall be grasped by a faith that is really living. New religions, the experience of a generation has now made clear, are vital enough: they seize one by the throat. Prophets they hardly need—them they have aplenty. What they do demand is thoughtful criticism. They need reminding, lest their earnest striving be too new, lest they painfully forget what men have learned from the long line of inspired prophets of the past. Much of Europe has recently seemed one vast forgetting. And how much do our own flourishing churches really remember?

The great religions scarcely needed to seek primitive strength at all costs. The religions of civilizations that have developed a science and a philosophy have managed to incorporate that science into their values. They have identified their organization of religious values with their organization of intellectual values. The principle of intelligibility in that science has become "what all men call God." The religion of the priest, the religion of the prophet, and the religion of the healer have been held together by the theologian, because he has known God. These religions are in our world no longer so united, and threaten to go their separate ways. If we truly know God, if the reflective and intelligent consideration in the light of human experience of the ends of life and of the possibilities of nature takes on meaning once more, then the celebration and clarification of values will no longer be in opposition to their extension to all men. "This is life eternal, that they should know thee the only true God." What is needed is not the priest of a sentimental aestheticism, nor the prophet of an unimaginative social reform, nor the preacher of a popular uplift, nor even the professor of religion, but the theologian. And not the desperate apologist, seeking at all costs to prove that God exists, but the theologian, who really knows God and can make clear to us what he is.

For the history of religious thinking makes plain that the role of science and intelligence in religion is not the finding of new and better demonstrations *that* God is, but the continued criticism and purification of *what* God is, of what are the supreme values that are to organize our lives and give them significance. We have plenty of priests, plenty of prophets, plenty of counselors, plenty of apologists and reconcilers. Is there in our religious life no place left for theologians? for knowing God, for clarifying his attributes? For theologians who could tell us whether they are really exhausted in the *Hakenkreuz,* or the Hammer and Sickle, or the American flag, or the American Way of Life?

What are the values we really want to achieve by our busy religious techniques? What is the "true God"?

If we must accept the fact that our American religion, whatever its rites and symbols, is rapidly becoming a form of social and moral idealism under a thin veneer of religious language, what then is the contribution of scientific method and intelligent criticism to determining what is the true moral ideal? If what religion does, its function (which we can hardly hope to abolish, or transform, or even alter), is to strengthen commitment to our living faith by consecrating the genuine values of our own group, then the primary role of science and knowledge in the religious life is to clarify through intelligence the values to which we are actually consecrated. And in that process we may even hope to extend and enlarge and deepen our vision of the Divine.

Index

143